Blessed Wishes

Michael Harris

Killing a Colored Man's Pedigree

A Chronicled Exposé of an Endangered Species
The Black American Family

Michael Harrison

ISBN 978-1-64299-495-7 (hardcover)
ISBN 978-1-64299-494-0 (digital)

Christian Faith Publishing, Inc.
832 Park Avenue
Meadville, PA 16335
www.christianfaithpublishing.com

Printed in the United States of America

MICHAEL HARRISON

To those who are gone yet still keep me
connected to my own pedigree:
Terry C. Harrison Sr. and Emma S. Harrison
Terry C. Harrison Jr.
Arthur Gasaway and Ruby Gasaway
Spencer Blain Harrison, who was not destined to remain part of our
universe at this time but who may return someday another way

Contents

Acknowledgments

I would like to express much appreciation and gratitude for my astounding wife, Lynne, who has always inspired me forward with her love and support and who first told me years ago that I should write a book, although at that time neither of us knew what the subject should be.

I also thank my two daughters, Terri and Pia, for their love, support, and hours of typing. I thank my mother, Autherine Gasaway Harrison Lennon Quillian, who carried me into the physical part of this life. I also thank the rest of my family for their support.

I also wish to thank the team at Christian Faith Publishing, especially my agent, Linda Hewlett, for her many words of support and encouragement. I also wish to thank my editing supervisor, Mary Jones, for her help, patience, and walking me through the editing process.

I give my deepest and most personal note of gratitude to God for bringing my existence into this universe long enough for me to discover this destiny and the ones in the future.

Introduction

My Purpose in This Book

Before you turn the page, be warned: I have strong opinions, and my purpose in *Killing a Colored Man's Pedigree* is to examine how the extremely high unwed birthrate in the black community—nearly 73 percent as of 2017—is destroying black culture in America. I also offer practical solutions black people can employ to reverse this self-destructive trend.

As far as I'm concerned, this situation is nothing short of a cultural Armageddon. If this 70 percent–plus figure grows larger, I fear a cultural collapse that would place black America in a permanent underclass far more detrimental than the second-class status we held before the civil rights movement of the 1960s.

I'm a married black father, an exception to the apparent rule, but this situation still affects me as a black man. It also negatively affects the United States of America as a whole. The good news is, this problem exists because of cultural deficiencies within the greater black community, not because of racial ethnicity or any so-called superiority within any particular group.

This problem not only results in the inferior socioeconomic status that plagues a large part of the black community, it also feeds the high levels of AIDS and other sexually transmitted diseases that undermine a healthy culture. After all, unprotected sex is necessary in order to maintain a high unwed birthrate. Not surprisingly, the transference of AIDS/HIV infections has doubled in the black community since the early 1990s. In my home state of Georgia, blacks make up 78 percent of the AIDS cases diagnosed within the past several years.

The fact is, the gradual elimination of intact, two-parent black families slowly destroys the constructive lineage of the family tree, resulting in a weaker society within our own culture and producing a black community that eventually destroys the culture of its people.

The family cannot long survive without the patriarch and the matriarch. The human propagation of married individuals provides a succession of generations that preserves the integrity of lineage and genealogy. In other words, these are the seeds that plant the family tree. Within the black community, the family tree is dying at the roots and being replaced by groups that consist of a mother and some siblings who often don't even share the same last name.

Unfortunately, this situation is further exacerbated by our present lack of black leadership. Most current black leaders are too corrupt to speak truthfully and are devoid of the integrity possessed by past black leaders. Even the duplicitous propagandized Million Man March of the 1990s produced nugatory results because its mission never addressed the root cause of the problem in black America.

For the record, please let me state that my opinion on this subject does not come from a position of self-righteous judgment. Members of my own family have children out of wedlock, and I grew up in a home broken by the divorce of my own parents, both of whom lived out their respective childhoods in broken families. The children of my siblings likewise have fallen victims to the problems of divorce and separation from their own fathers.

As a teenager and young adult, I too displayed similar self-destructive behaviors. With the aid of professional analysis, I realized I did not wish to pass this unhealthy pattern onto my own children. I have come to understand that, in most cases, married people produce children who become married adults, divorced people produce children who become divorced adults, and single people produce children who become unwed parents. The cycle of this fatherless epidemic continues and spreads because these behaviors are learned.

In my own family, my father's father had no brothers; my father, who is deceased, was an only child; I am his only child; and I have no sons. This means I am the last Harrison in my family, and when I am gone, there will be no more.

This gives me a strange feeling about the overall condition in black America. Since it is obviously too late for me to continue my own name, perhaps I can put forth a message that in some small way might help preserve black American family culture. Hopefully, this message will improve the situation for my daughters, whose lives are infinitely more important, precious, and valuable to me than my own.

Because black people are the only ethnic group in this country that did not originally come to America via the natural voluntary process of immigration, we do not know our lineage or the name of our forefathers in Africa. How ironic that our current modern behavior mimics this same tragedy. We who bear children today are the forefathers of the generations to come. Will they, too, lack a lineage and family tree?

No racial group is superior to any other, but because of our own immoral behavior, black Americans are creating an inferior culture of people. This situation is causing the among realization of black people with no consistent blood line, a race of mutts with no pedigree and no breeding.

Black people must change this present course of destruction and produce within our community a new demographic of thinkers, not panderers; a new generation of leaders, not followers; and ultimately a community of more marketers and acquirers, not only consumers.

Many black people accept the status quo because it is convenient. Many of us pretend to be unaware of what this cultural disaster really means because fixing it presents too great a challenge. But I believe it was the great Frederick Douglas who told us, "Sometimes, struggle is a necessary process of progress."

You'll see my own struggle in the pages of this book. What I write here isn't politically correct. Nonetheless, I've written this book because I feel I must speak out in the face of such dangerous silence. I hope this book and its easily verified facts can help in some small way to turn the tide and encourage my fellow black Americans to do their part to rescue black American culture before it's too late.

1

Setting the Stage

As I stated in the introduction, as of 2017, the unwed birthrate for black Americans was about 73 percent. Contrast that with white America in which the unwed birthrate for the same year was 27 percent (about 52 percent of unmarried Latino women occupy this same statistic). In 2017, the total number of unmarried births in the United States reached an all-time high of 40 percent. This means that single mothers are raising more than 25 million American children. Between 2005 and 2015, the number of unmarried mothers increased by 5 percent. This trend began years ago and has continued through 2017 based on data monitored by the US census bureau and the Center for Health Statistics of CDC.

The trouble doesn't end there: research shows that few single mothers marry after bearing an illegitimate child. In fact, having a child out of wedlock appears to significantly decrease a woman's chances of ever marrying, by as much as 30 percent in some estimates.

These astonishing figures mean the great majority of black babies born in the US today will grow up to become a population of black adults who will function—or dysfunction—outside the mental and social structure of the two-parent monogamous family unit.

The gradual disintegration of this nuclear family structure is the root cause of all the negative statistics that plague the black community: the high black unemployment rate, the high percentage of black male incarceration, the relatively low number of black college graduates, the higher black high school dropout rate, and a higher level of black poverty.

In recent years, I have also noticed an interesting phenomenon: a growing social trend of lower-class single Caucasian women with children who appear to be fathered by black men. In most cases, these women return to the black community to raise their fatherless offspring, where they are more likely to be accepted. They dare not return to suburban middle class white America with these black babies for fear of condemnation, judgment, and ostracism.

In my opinion, these children are damaged twice: they often feel the outcast status of an indefinite racial identity and they have no paternal identity. They sometimes subconsciously believe themselves to be bastards both of their family and of their own ethnicity. I must say I find it a strange irony that there are some white women who have become willing conspirators and participants in the genocide of the Negro pedigree.

Nonetheless, since these problems are ultimately self-inflicted, they can only be solved from within the black community. We black people must save ourselves from the future of destruction that comes from years of unwed breeding. To turn this situation around, we must start asking ourselves the unasked questions, such as why are there no great black leaders today who inspire us to improve our present national fatherless condition? After all, most of the great black leaders of the past were produced from backgrounds of strong patriarchal influence. A brief look at the past helps explain what's going on.

In the 1940s and 1950s, there were many blacks who occupied factory, construction, and other domestic jobs in the cities. Others occupied rural and farm communities in the south. These individuals appeared to have overcome the past status quo of separation from their loved ones that occurred when their great-grandparents were sold away from their families during slavery, a situation some sociologists believe explains the lingering existence of so many black single-parent homes today. Most of these blacks belonged to two-parent working-class families, resulting in a positive, energetic black population and a similar type of black leader.

This blue-collar black population with a strong family structure and an equally strong work ethic disappeared from the black community when these domestic and factory jobs moved to the white population or were outsourced to third-world countries.

In the face of this change, blacks tended to remain in the city without good jobs. Desperation began to grow, and the single unwed black birthrate began its initial ascent. These blacks were influenced by a media that in turn was controlled by a narrow monopoly. This manipulated media market fed an inner-city single-mother culture looking for instant self-gratification and resulted in the kind of population unlikely to produce leaders who would sacrifice themselves to achieve a productive common goal.

Still, in the 1950s and 1960s, the unwed birthrate among black Americans was only about 7 percent. That means this number has grown at a steady rate of about 1.6 percent per year.

But back to the 1960s. This was when the government began giving welfare only to those families that could prove there was no adult male means of support in the home. While not a deliberate effort to destroy black families, this was indeed one of the many failed liberal democrat political policies that are never ever thought through in a thorough manner.

Of course, I realize a high unwed birthrate exists elsewhere in the world besides black America. In the United States, a group of seventeen white teenage girls at Gloucester High School in Massachusetts started a pregnancy club in 2008. The basis of the club? Agreeing to all become pregnant at the same time and raise their babies as single mothers together. There are reality TV shows on air such as "16 and pregnant" and "Teen Mom" which subliminally glorify teenage pregnancy. In some European countries with a large majority white population and a largely secular culture, a huge percentage of children are growing up in non-married homes. However, in the better developed countries of Africa, for example, the unwed birthrate is low because of African social and religious culture.

Contrast such trends with the American Jewish community, in which the divorce rate is about the same as the US national average, but the unwed birthrate is almost nonexistent. There may be some degree of dysfunction in Jewish families, but their devout religious culture is completely non-accepting of unwed pregnancies.

Likewise, in the Asian community in the United States and abroad, the divorce rate and unwed birthrate are both less than 1%. Asian culture mandates a strongly regimented two-parent family structure since this best facilitates the child's academic success. This is why Asian students score much higher than blacks, whites, or Latinos on standardized math and science tests as evidenced by Charles Murray's and Richard J. Herrnstein's Bell Curve theory that talks about cognitive stratification. Based upon data monitored by the United States Bureau of Labor statistics, Asians are the highest income earning demographic group in the U.S. It is now an average of about 85 thousand dollars a year and I don't think this is coincidental.

I once came across a survey taken from American high school students in which a specific question asked, "What is the lowest grade your parents would accept you bringing home?" The question was asked of public school students from middle-class backgrounds made up of three different ethnic groups: white, black, and Asian. And the results were telling.

Most of the Asian students answered, "My parents would accept nothing less than an A." Most white students answered, "My parents would accept a B or a C." About 70 percent of the black students answered, "My mom said as long as I pass it's okay" or that their parents did not care. The child's achievement or lack of achievement becomes a self-fulfilling prophecy. It depends upon what the parents expect of them.

Children learn to expect from themselves what is expected of them. Many low-performing children are only late bloomers or they have emotional problems that hinder their learning ability. Most of them would do very well if they had a better environment.

Black people need to learn critical lessons from these other cultures. In the black community, we have come to a point where a high divorce rate would be an improvement over what we have currently. In a short period of time, historically speaking, black Americans bypassed the divorce statistic and regressed to before civilization began, when humans mated indiscriminately and had babies without the benefits of the institution of marriage.

We black people must remind ourselves that producing children within the confines of marriage is part of what separates humans from lower animal species. Even if a marriage does end in divorce, children have a better chance of maintaining a legal contact or a relationship with both parents after divorce than if the father is not present or acknowledged at all.

This brings me to two fundamental questions: how have we come to this sorry state, and how do we correct it? In the following chapters, I attempt to answer both these questions.

2

Value of the Alpha Male

The high unwed birth rate among blacks and the resulting behavior can be easier to understand when we take a closer look at some theories put forth by social and behavioral scientists. These theories examine psychological behavior in human beings but become even more enlightening when the social behaviors of other mammals are taken into account.

For example, scientists have learned that male mammals can only imitate normal male behavior that has been observed from the alpha male. This is because male mammal behavior is typically learned whereas female mammal behavior tends to be instinctive.

This fact is so important that when the alpha male is absent, the behavioral development of the beta male often becomes retarded in some way. In turn, this is because the primal nature of the male brain is hardwired to be aggressive and territorial, behavior that can only be civilized by repetitive and routine exposure to a civilized alpha male.

To determine this fact of male mammal life, scientists conducted experiments on primates in which one male baby chimpanzee was raised in a native physical natural environment populated by female chimpanzees only. This baby male chimp was not allowed to interact with any other male chimps until he reached maturity.

Upon reaching maturity, he was introduced to a population of normal males, but he displayed quite an abnormal behavior. Sometimes he became very withdrawn and tried to isolate himself from the other males and cover himself with his limbs. Sometimes, he displayed sudden and unpredictable violent outbursts. At other times, he demonstrated the physical mannerisms of female primate social behavior. In response, some of his male neighbors ostracized him while other males became belligerent and made violent gestures toward him.

A similar experiment was conducted in which a baby chimp was taken from its mother at birth and deprived of physical contact with apes or humans until it reached maturity. It's only contact occurred during feeding. Once it reached maturity, it too was reintegrated with a simian population. Not surprisingly, its behavior was similar to that of the first chimp that was deprived of male interaction.

Scientists recently made a related discovery while studying the possible future extinction of the African elephant, whose social behavior and intelligence level is closer to humans than even that of lower primates. For example, elephants experience fear, love, anger, and posttraumatic shock syndrome on the same level as humans. Somewhat territorial but docile creatures unless provoked or threatened, they never initiate aggression against another animal species, yet several herds of young African male elephants were observed randomly attacking and murdering nearby hippopotamus and rhinoceros for no apparent reason, and some random human attacks occurred as well.

At first, scientists could find no reason for such senseless and absurd behavior on the part of the young elephants, but then they started asking what factor these elephants had in common. It was learned that all these males had witnessed the brutal and violent murders of their parents by human hunters and poachers when they were babies.

Somehow, the ones that managed to survive on their own, orphaned and alone, grew into young adulthood without learning elephant social behavior from other adults. Observation also showed that they reached sexual maturity much too early in their development.

As an experiment, scientists transplanted several large adult bull elephants from other regions into the herds of young violent males, and the effect was almost immediate: the young males' violent aggression disappeared, and they eventually migrated to and successfully integrated into other herds.

Other telling behavioral experiments have been conducted for the purpose of proving or disproving the accuracy of the Oedipus complex in species other than human. Sigmund Freud's famous theory states that one's choice of mate is determined by one's relationship with his or her opposite gender parent.

A group of scientists conducted an experiment in which female sheep gave birth to ten male sheep and female goats gave birth to ten male goats. The ten male baby sheep were taken away from their mothers at birth and given to the mother goats to raise while the ten male baby goats were taken away from their mothers at birth and given to the mother sheep to raise.

Once all twenty male animals reached maturity, they were integrated into an environment with twenty adult females, ten goats and ten sheep, that were ready to mate. The results were telling: the male goats refused to mate with the female goats. They would only mate with the female sheep. Likewise, all ten male sheep refused the female sheep and instead would mate only with the female goats.

This same experiment was conducted with female baby goats and sheep, but the results were more varied and inconclusive at the rate of about 50/50 each way.

Instructive zoological studies have also been done on the social behavior of animals such as the African zebra. For example, scientists followed several groups of zebras for many months before they fully understood what heretofore had seemed to be puzzling behavior.

Each group always consisted of one adult alpha male, between one and three adult alpha females, one or two adult subordinate females, and one to three baby zebras. The curious behavior was that the adult male would mate only with the alpha females, and mating with the alpha male was their only function within the group.

The subordinate females were always ignored by the alpha males, and these females' only function was caring for and feeding the baby zebras. Sometimes, an adult male stranger would approach the group for the purpose of mating with one of the subordinate females, but the alpha male always turned violently on the new male and chased him off.

The alpha male clearly did not want the subordinate females for himself, but he would not allow them to mate with anyone else unless he was first defeated in a fight. Only then did he allow the subordinate females to leave with the new male.

Zoologists followed these and other groups of zebras for several months before they learned that the subordinate females were the daughters of the alpha male. He was protecting his lineage by letting his daughters mate only with males with a proven superior pedigree.

Different types of premating rituals are performed by various species of animals, but the purpose is always the same: to determine the superior males. In certain species of birds, for example, an adult female will perform a mating dance to attract the attention of several adult males. Each male will respond by constructing a nest. When the nests are complete, the female will examine each one and test it for size and strength. She then mates with the male who has built the largest and strongest nest.

Such premating rituals were designed by nature to match females from the most superior gene pool with the most superior males in order to perpetuate the strongest DNA in that species.

The system works pretty well throughout most of the animal kingdom—until human behavior is examined and a failure rate enters the equation. To put it bluntly, the human female is the only animal that will mate with an inferior human male.

Black women complain that no good black men are available to choose from, but most available black men have been raised by single women without the benefit of a civilized alpha male inside the home to observe and imitate. Therefore, women are complaining about a problem they themselves created.

It is unfair for women to complain about the behavior of men when they continuously exercise poor taste in men. This is the area in which the father/daughter relationship becomes critically important. The function of the alpha male in his daughter's life is to provide an example of the best possible mate for herself and best possible father for her children. In his son's life, the alpha male's function is to model the type of behavior his son should mimic.

Civilized behavior in the human male animal simply does not develop from the daily and yearly exposure to a single mother. Instead, it develops from the young male's subconscious fear of the physical threat and presence of the civilized alpha male. Whenever a young male hears the heavier bass tone in the alpha male's voice, he learns to respect and fear the role model of authority. In other words, the voice of the alpha male suppresses the compulsive impulse of recalcitrant behavior. There is simply no substitute for this lesson; it is vital for the civil development of the male.

It becomes mentally and emotionally impossible for the young male to fear the female because of the softer treble tone of her voice. As time passes and the young male grows larger in size and strength, he develops his own bass tone. As he becomes more accustomed to the deeper tone of his own voice, he becomes less intimidated by and more indifferent to the treble octave of his mother's voice.

Typically, when this male human mammal grows large enough to feel the increased difference in his own physical strength, he undertakes some type of physical challenge with a testosterone-laden alpha male. This is how he learns the limitations of self-control, without which he develops abnormal, out-of-control behaviors.

This is why single women who raise male children eventually lose control of them and young fatherless males typically begin to exhibit the behavior of the absent alpha male syndrome. Often, as with the fatherless elephants, this behavior manifests itself through anger or violence. Allow me to give an anecdotal, non-hypothetical example of this point. In Atlanta, Georgia, on Christmas night, 2008, two such barbaric savages, the spawn of two baby mamas, carjacked an innocent old lady. After snatching her from her vehicle, they ran over her with her own car. Fortunately, she survived with two broken legs.

Also during the summer of 2009, a twelve-year-old boy murdered his one-month-old baby cousin while sitting in a car in a department store parking lot while his single mother was shopping inside. Another example, later that summer, two other worthless individuals committed a home burglary. They shot a young mother and beat her one-year-old baby son unconscious. After these two were captured by the law, the news media interviewed the single mother of one of these two individuals. During the interview, she asked the viewing TV audience to pray for her son.

I will pray for her son. I will pray for him to spend the next fifty years in a cage like the animal he is. In the summer of 2016, in my own neighborhood, some carjacking thug ran over and killed an innocent grandmother and her two grandchildren while they were walking home from church, all while fleeing from the police. In May of 2017, Madison County, Mississippi, one of these unmarried baby mamas left her five-year-old son alone in the car of a grocery store parking lot. Three criminal animals, the spawns of some other baby mamas, stole the car and murdered the child. We as black people only make up about 13 percent of the US population, but we commit about 38 percent of all the violent street crimes. This is disgraceful. The aforementioned examples I gave you are but a small sample of the destruction and violence perpetrated by the inhumane monsters on and on through till the present day. In America, there are generations of young black fatherless males growing up to become these uncivilized unmanageable misfits. These kinds of robberies, murders, rapes, shootings, and various other types of violent crimes happen each and every day in my city of Atlanta and all across this country. The only common denominator is that more than 90 percent of these crimes are perpetrated by some predatory animal that was originally downloaded and raised by some single mother. Most of them seem to always have some stereotypical, ghetto-sounding, fake afro-centric name like Devarquarious, Laquantavious, or Shareed Jamocha Fudge Muhammad Quadruple X Jr.

If you want to give your child an African, Russian, or even a Norwegian name, that's fine, but why not actually use your brain, do some research, and look up the real names of those national origins?

I am quite willing to play devil's advocate, and I realize that ax murderers and serial killers do come from two-parent homes, but one unmarried female parent is not an acceptable substitute for two bad married parents.

In fact, I'm willing to bet that the most dangerous monster that can be released upon civilized society is the human male animal raised by a neurotic single female. I am convinced this is where the greater percentage of our rapists and most violent sociopaths and murderers are manufactured and cultivated.

We black Americans cannot allow these abnormal and other social practices of fatherless children to become our zeitgeist. As the father of two daughters, this prospect frightens me. With so few psychologically healthy males left in the black community, there may soon be no menu from which black women can make a quality selection of a future husband, a prospect that alarms and saddens me more than I can say.

3

Evolution of an
Endangered Species

If we broaden the examination of the present status of black America, specifically the black male, you will discover that what is happening in the black community is but a mere microcosm of what is occurring in American society as a whole. Just as the black family is an endangered species, so is the totality of American masculinity.

Going back to the middle eighteenth century, the American male image was somewhat puritanical and Victorian in its presentation of the prudishly refined and polite patriarch who valued integrity and honor.

But if the modern twenty-first century man wishes to exist in the present antagonistic politically correct environment, he must include a lifestyle that encompasses roles that were traditionally held by women at home and at work.

For quite some time, that manipulated media monopoly that I mentioned in chapter one has often predicted the future peril of manhood. There may be some validity to these prognostications.

As the American economy has changed from manual labor to a more technology-based workforce over the past thirty years, more women are working. Men's portion of the labor force has decreased from 70 percent in the mid-1940s to less than 50 percent now. In our major cities, single young women without children earn almost 10 percent more money than their male counterparts. Women equal or surpass men as a percentage of college students and undergraduates while men still outnumber women in substance abuse, homelessness, suicide, and violent criminality. If you include our recent bad economy, which has damaged our more traditionally male-dominated jobs, it explains why anthropological scholars fear the future prospect of the American man. But if so many experts believe that American manhood is in so much trouble, how do we fix this problem? Since no one knows the answer to that question, some men have returned to the decorum of customs past for redemption.

Professors from Harvard and Rutgers University believe men should embrace a more aggressive approach by taking on a more synthetic or cosmetic style of masculinity. This idea would take on the appearance of the successful urban male wearing the attire of the rugged outdoorsman for example. This concept could look like a more acceptable version of a passive-aggressive type of masculinity, like the retail-clothing store Nordstrom's designer fake muddy blue jeans or actor Tim Allen's TV show, *Last Man Standing*. This fictitious kind of maleness is passed off as a substitute by our new popular culture. These examples seem to expand beyond ethnicity and socioeconomic backgrounds. Some believe that if we expect men to remain with these stale definitions of manhood, it only keeps the problem alive. There are those who would say that this forces men to face new issues the same way that they handled old ones: by holding women responsible or using "hanging out with the guys" excuse or hiding their fears behind some other form of exaggerated virility. This does nothing to help them do better in school, maintain better jobs, or become good fathers in an economic climate that is moving away from the commercial image of masculinity. The fact is, it's not how men fashion their appearance that makes them complete; it's how they behave in their day-to-day activities.

But please allow this brief digression to the evolutionary portion of this analysis:

By the end of the eighteenth and early nineteenth century, the American male had progressed to a manually skilled worker (a farmer, carpenter, shoemaker, etc.). This new American man has a more punitive view of the European males' preoccupation with his stylish attire. These nineteenth-century men saw themselves as independent thinkers whose mission was to conquer the American western landscape. By the end of the nineteenth century, these men who were blacksmiths and shoemakers were evolving into storekeepers and manufacturers of goods and services. They sought to become men whose level of development and achievement depended upon their ability to compete in the free market's enterprise of ideas.

Now back to the present: the construction workers, plumbers, and electricians of the past did not wear their work clothes to make themselves feel manlier. Their self-defined purpose of masculinity came from their own practical usefulness to the public service industry. The belief that masculinity is a role that one portrays reduces ones' manhood to a cosmetic decoration. It's like saying that a woman's femininity is defined based on how much makeup she wears. The personification of American womanhood has gone through several changes over the past five or six decades, but the self-defined male image has not changed that much, even if some men now believe that there are fewer chances to advance or satisfy their ambitions. The consequence is that men have two options: they can feel as though they don't fulfill the necessary standards, or they have to become a lot more imaginative.

That means that the necessary course of action is to free themselves from the past, not to reunite with it, not a restoration of the old role, but a broadened interpretation of it. The end of manliness isn't near, and machismo is not dead. But its meaning should be expanded to include the tough side and the softer side. In other words, it's time for a new kind of masculinity, a new vision of what is expected of male behaviors in two different domains, home and work. That has always decided their value. Sometimes that's not as easy to do as it sounds. American culture is competitive and traditional, which is different from popular culture, which is less so. There are reasons why urban fathers, stockbrokers, and company executives aren't taking more time off work to take care of the children or pursuing new careers like nursing, a field where few men of today consider.

Most men don't believe they need to be rescued from a lack of choices because they still dominate the career numbers as politicians and in the corporate arena, earn more money in business and in the movie box office, and still do less housework.

But these gaps between women and men in pay earnings are due to people's personal choices, not some conspiratorial or overt effort of sexism or male chauvinism against women. Although there are more women in college than men, men still pursue more advanced and graduate degrees in math and science, whereas women still pursue more liberal arts degrees. Women also work fewer hours because they use more maternity leave and time off for childcare. But again, these are personal choices. As for the motion picture and movie-making industry, the economic numbers are driven by the supply and demand and free market choices of movie viewing and audiences. In fact, legendary 1950s movie star Elizabeth Taylor was the first actor in movie-making industry history to be paid one million dollars for her performance in the movie *Cleopatra* in the early 1960s. That amount of money is nothing by today's standards, but it was a fortune back in those days.

Back to the evolutionary digression: During the later part of the nineteenth century and early part of the twentieth century, the blue-collar factory workers in manufacturing during the industrial revolution combined with the self-made men in continuing to build the country.

Now back to the present: The competition between the genders causes casualties on both sides. When men lose, it hurts women and children also. Because as women begin to move into positions that were once only held by men, and more male divisions of the American economy becomes smaller, a larger, more opportunistic expectation of manhood may be required. This may be an essential for America and its men to match its international rivals in this new millennium. An obvious place to start would be in the home. When men spend more time at home performing daily chores with the kids, they receive much accolade. Women never get that kind of praise for the same activity because historically, societal standards for men are still somewhat low. Today's modern family practices haven't changed that much. Even with the great progress our society has made in equality, the wife still does much more of the housework and childcare than the husband. Even when the man is unemployed, the woman still does more at home. Also, in America, the number of fatherless homes is three times higher than the early 1960s and stay-at-home fathers now are about 3 percent.

Now back to the digressive part of this chapter: During the beginning of the twentieth century, the feeling of ill-being from years of factory-worker burnout influences the American male to begin a fatherhood agenda as a means to fabricate manhood in their sons.

Back to the present: In the 1990s, in some European countries, parts of Asia, and Australia, the government allowed parents to divide more than one year's worth of paid maternity leave between them. This was done as an effort to legislate men to spend more time as fathers and less time as workers. In those countries, their society has produced a new generation of men who feel pressured to comply. The United Sates is now the only industrialized country that does not have a similar law. But change may be coming. Politicians on both the left and right are increasingly moving toward the support for some kind of paid paternity leave. Big companies with large male workforces are beginning to offer these benefits of some sort, and more states are considering such legislation. But government policy cannot always change societal perceptions. California was the first state to finance six weeks' leave for both parents, but only about 25 percent of men took advantage compared to 75 percent women. Men always took less time no matter what. Taking more time off for babies is still not considered the manly thing to do. Yet thus far, the US federal budget has allocated millions of dollars to help the individual states to operate their own paid family leave program.

Now back to the further progress of the male evolution: As we moved through the first half of the twentieth century, the American man begins to focus more on the appearance of his physique as women begin to occupy more of the workplace.

Fast forward, back to the present: Of the several million job opportunities that have evolved over the past decade, most of them came from areas that attracted more women than men. Men occupy only about 16 percent of the job titles that have grown over the past decade. Those were accountants and construction workers. The rest include teachers, registered nurses, home health aids, and customer service reps, all at about a half million new positions each, and mostly women. The social division of the American economy have projected an increase of about seven million jobs by 2018. But unless the demographic of the workforce changes, about two and a half million of them may not be filled according to research done by Northwestern University. The potential employment gap might symbolize big opportunities for working-class men and the families they're trying to support. The dilemma is that men, unlike many women, still feel confined to a narrow scope of adequate masculine functions, and that sphere of reach hasn't kept stride with the changing employment opportunities. As manufacturing jobs continue to move overseas and illegal immigrants continue to provide cheap manual labor, American men continue to fall behind.

As the evolution of the American male moves further into the middle of the twentieth century, the post-World War 2 man becomes a bit consumed by corporate capitalism as he becomes the stronger family provider, and the self-made man makes a comeback from the nineteenth century to conquer modern suburbia as more American men enjoy being single and unattached.

Back to the present: The recession of the last decade has only exacerbated the course and direction of the American male falling behind in the workforce. Historically, women are usually the ones who totally abdicate the labor force after losing their jobs. But now men are beginning to gain ground in this area. About one and a half million men switched from "looking for jobs" to "stopped looking" in one month periods during the extremely non-productive Obama years. Deprived of confidence, hope, or spirit by the scarcity of "manly" work, they just gave up. High school and college graduates were even worse off. The unemployment rate among young men was over 20 percent, which was three points higher than their female counterparts, and these numbers are much higher in the black community. The US trade policies are imposed on foreign competitors to protect domestic producers, and immigration laws do protect blue-collar jobs to some degree, but the United States can't stop this practice altogether. If the American male is to maintain his positive self-image and the American economy remain healthy, the next generation of middle-class family men will have to stop looking for outsourced manufacturing jobs and start exploring positions that are traditionally held by women. In order to speed up this change in process, schools that train in these professions should start an energetic and enterprising recruitment programs to target young males. Change of this nature is already occurring on its own. According to the Bureau of Labor Statistics, the number of male nurses has doubled over the past thirty years to about 8 percent, and there are more male elementary schoolteachers too, but not enough.

Back to US male evolution: As we move closer toward the end of the twentieth century, the image of the ruthless corporate capitalist grows as the American male manipulates hedge funds and dominates the stock market as greed becomes the new ambition. As far as my personal opinion goes, I have held the belief for a long time that our present-day society has this conspiracy to undermine masculinity in American culture. I see this being done through the propagandized messaging in our 90 percent-plus liberal media, our 90 percent-plus liberal entertainment industry, and our 90 percent-plus liberal public government education system. These entities constantly blur the descriptive lines between male and female by implying that they are both the same under the phony façade of equality.

Case in point: An Obama policy requires public schools to allow boys to use girls' bathrooms and locker rooms under the guise of a dubious transgender law. Hopefully this law can be successfully rescinded on a Federal level by President Trump, but in some local and state governments, this policy is being promoted, including my home state of Georgia. Also in my hometown of Atlanta, some local municipalities and school boards require gender quizzes to be taken by sixth graders in the public school system. And our latest example is we no longer have the Boy Scouts organization; it is now the Girl Boy Scouts. When I was a boy, this—what used to be a great organization—served me quite well growing up without a father. I suppose I'm fortunate this new policy didn't exist when I was a boy. I also thank God my daughters are adults and can no longer be victims of the public school system.

Women and men are equal, but they are definitely not the same. They are quite different physically, biologically, mentally, and emotionally.

Based on what is visible to the naked eye, today's modern male version of masculinity has driven men further away from their traditional role, and they have withdrawn to their man cave or to more recreational outdoor activities. This modern-day man feels more inside conflict and self-contradiction; ergo, he must divide himself between being a provider and a stay-at-home dad. Generally speaking, if the male mentality becomes less superficial, and more men engage the idea of parental leave, women would not bear as much of the load. If more men were more involved with their children, especially black men, more kids would excel in school and fewer kids might become involved in crime and become more prosperous, spiritually, and emotionally healthy adults.

4

Phony Victim Status—a Modern Copout for Blacks

I know my position on this subject will offend men and women alike, but I maintain that no woman can claim victim status if she makes the voluntary choice to have unprotected, casual sex with the wrong man, who then leaves her with a disease or an illegitimate pregnancy. The only victim in such a situation is the fatherless child, who suffers the consequences, carries the burden, and pays the price for the intentional, promiscuous actions of its irresponsible mother.

Unfortunately, claiming victim status is rampant in black American culture, and it has some surprising and negative results. I would like to offer one particular story to illustrate this point.

When my eldest daughter was a student at one of our nation's predominately black universities, she informed me that the college she attended had an on-campus child daycare facility for female students with children. I found this very disturbing, but what she added frightened me even more: the young women were allowed to bring their children to class. You can just imagine the type of disruption of what is supposed to be a learning environment.

I ask, "How is this development good for the black community, the other students who are trying to learn, or the credibility of the university?"

Would this type of practice be tolerated at a predominately white university such as Notre Dame, Georgia Tech, or Stanford? If it were, would you want your child to attend this college?

My daughter also informed me that just before the last presidential election, one of her college professors threatened to lower the grade of any student who could not provide proof that they had cast a ballot voting for Obama. After I advised my daughter to inform this instructor that this request was highly unethical and quite possibly illegal, this professor backed down and changed her mind.

Please excuse that digression from my central point, but my purpose is to illustrate that these are clear examples of life in a mental institution in which the patients are in charge.

As black people, we also choose to languish in the problems of society such as welfare, war, and high prices to further project the false conspiratorial victimization unto ourselves. We then continue to wallow in this anxiety, which preoccupies one's ability to function in relationships that are healthy enough to lead to marriage. It is true that we live and exist in a world with many problems and much moral decline. But we also have more available opportunities than any previous generations, yet we don't take advantage of them. These are issues that should be resolved before one brings children into the world.

Before you can become the qualified half of a two-parent family, you have to grow and become a whole mature happy person yourself. And happiness is something you have to find inside yourself. Happiness is not an external thing. There is no possession or person that can make you happy unless you learn to be content with your own solitude first. An example of that would be the many show business performers who need the constant adulation and sounds of cheering applause to make them feel happy. As soon as they leave the stage, they feel lonely, sad, and depressed even though they have fame and wealth.

These people never learned how to be happy with or by themselves before they acquired so much external gratification. If a person has not learned to be satisfied with his or her own alone existence, then he or she has no reservoir of love to give anyone. That ability is a confirmation of one's own maturation and growth. Black people have also allowed themselves to buy into external examples of despair like this so-called global climate change pollution. But the damage we have done to ourselves is much worse and more dangerous than what might happen to the environment.

We make excuses to justify our own bad behavior by saying it's okay because I'm only human, I'm not perfect—but this is just another copout. Some people convince themselves that the only two options are to do what is wrong or be perfect. Perfection is not a reality that was meant to be achieved inside any human person. Perfection in its defined context can be created by a person in an inanimate object or a work of art. For a righteous person, the afterlife might be perfect, but there is no perfect person, whatever that means. If there were such a person, he or she would be unbearably boring.

There is a healthy middle level of behavior between the extreme unrealistic expectation of perfection and catastrophe. But you have to become disciplined enough to make a conscious decision to take possession of your own integrity. That is what being a mature adult is about. One example of this point is that famous false slogan in the nutrition business that quotes: Diets don't work. This is a lie and another copout. Diets do work if the person disciplines him or herself to stay on the diet.

The true statement would be that some people on diets don't work.

They don't work hard enough on their eating behavior to stick with a diet of less food or fewer calories. But obviously, starving one's self doesn't work. Millions of people lose and maintain a normal healthy weight throughout their lifetime with a structured disciplined diet. You would never tell someone that alcohol and drug rehab don't work. Well, dieting is rehab for people whose drug is food.

Any person can find an excuse to have a substance abuse relapse, just as one could relapse with food. It's about controlling one's behavior, and that behavior may be about food, drugs, or even unprotected casual sex. Once we grow into adults, part of who we have become is that same child we used to be. Our personality is shaped by some of the same memories and experiences we had as a child. For those of us who felt or were abandoned by one of our parents, that experience becomes our adult reality and how we see the world.

We then subconsciously gravitate toward people who are likely to abandon us as adults, or we drive away people who really care with our own repelling behavior. You will never have a healthy relationship with someone until you force yourself to separate that damaged child from who you should have become by now as an adult. At the same time, you have to try and keep that happy childish part of yourself without being an immature adult. You have to learn to love yourself without confusing self-love with being self-indulgent, self-absorbed, selfish, or vain.

You must understand the difference. People who take their own adulthood too seriously all the time come across as being boring or sometimes threatening. One of the great things about marriage is that you can be many things to each other, even though a good healthy marriage is a very mature adult relationship. Husbands and wives can be each other's lovers, parents, partners, playmates, and friends. There are sometimes when a husband needs his wife to nurture him as a mother once did, and then there are sometimes when a wife needs to be comforted by her husband as her father once did.

These are concepts that are vanishing in the black community because the idea of sharing a life in marriage is portrayed to be less attractive than the single-parent lifestyle.

Look at my hometown of Atlanta, where a Single Mothers Convention was recently held a few years ago. I confess my first thought was to wonder how well the PC (politically correct) police would tolerate the notion of a married mother's convention! To my way of thinking, this entire idea discriminates against married mothers, yet it goes unchallenged. I ask, "Where are the support, praise, admiration, and commendations for married mothers?"

Equally bad black women were targeted by implication for this convention, even though no racial preference was apparent in the advertising so as not to stereotype black women or discriminate against single white mothers. For one thing, the convention was held at one of metro Atlanta's downtown convention centers, where the majority population is black. By contrast, the venues located in the surrounding counties of Atlanta away from the downtown area are where most of Atlanta's white population lives. In addition, TV promotions for the convention appeared to be sponsored by black community organizations, and radio advertisements and promotions were only broadcast on black radio stations.

A few months ago, the ABC television network conducted a Best Single Parent of the Year contest hosted by its popular daily morning news show. Again I ask, "Where is the award prize for the best married parents of the year?" The fact is that a cultural misconception exists that makes single mothers appear more glamorous, noble, and deserving of sympathy than married parents. The common belief is that raising children as a single mother is more difficult than raising them within a marriage.

This is not necessarily true, because our modern permissive culture gives unwed mothers the freedom to continue a recreational and social life with multiple dating partners, whereas raising children within a monogamous marriage requires more discipline and is more difficult. Married parents have to care for and nurture the children as well as maintain and nurture a healthy marriage. Divorced and widowed parents have their own unique issues, but studies show that when these parents date, they are more likely to be involved in a monogamous relationship even if it doesn't lead to marriage.

Making babies without a marital commitment should not be encouraged by society, but for many women, it is simply easier to birth a fatherless child than it is to become the kind of woman who will attract a husband. This child is then burdened with the curse and responsibility of providing its mother with the love and emotional gratification she is not getting from a man. Often, this woman's subliminal thought process is, "If no man will love me, this baby will have to."

If the baby is female, the mother has a lifelong built-in girlfriend. If the child is male, she has a live-in platonic boyfriend whom she can initially control, but this control is short-lived. As the child grows, he will begin to rebel against the lack of a two-parent family structure and no involvement of an alpha male. These women believe they have the right to have a baby. That is incorrect because no one has a right to someone else's life. You only have an obligation to protect the baby's right to have two married parents.

These are unfair burdens to place on a child and are also the cruelest forms of selfishness. Too many women refuse to be the kind of person a good and decent man will love and commit to. Instead, they just birth a baby whom they extract love from to meet their emotional needs. This entire process becomes a lesson in narcissism and phony victimization, and the same behaviors are transferred to the child. The child soon learns to become a self-absorbed adult, and the dysfunctional circle is complete.

One more reason that so many black people are such comfortable victims is their compliance with a liberal media's condescending promotion of racial stereotypes. For example: ABC News recently did a broadcast report on the dramatic increase in the number of single American women giving birth. Unfortunately, I became uncomfortable with how biased the report was aired. The only example and interview shown in the news report was that of the stereotypical black single woman with child.

I was offended as a black American because the report was not about single black women; it was about single American women. There should have been a Latino and Anglo woman also featured in this report to keep it accurately fair and balanced. I tried to dismiss this as coincidence, but I could not because I remembered a similar piece that aired several weeks earlier by the same network. That report was about how the bad US economy has affected American families. Again, there were four different families shown and interviewed.

All three of the families featured in the report contained white married couples with children, yet the only one so-called family shown with no male presence was a single black woman with a child. I have also seen other examples of these stereotypes extended beyond news media into TV shows and also TV commercial advertisement in which black women are stereotyped as being overweight or displaying a scary horse hair Halloween hairstyle that resembles Medusa, Raggedy Anne, or the original Bride of Frankenstein.

My main point here is to reveal how left-leaning mainstream liberal media networks expose themselves and their own patronizing style of racism by broadcasting news, entertainment, and market advertising to exploit appearances and implications of racial bigotry without being challenged. I have never seen these types of examples on the FOX network, and if there were any, I am sure there would be much outcry and protest from the liberal left.

Another firmly held belief of mine is that our large homeless population is in some ways connected to an absence of sound supportive parenting earlier in these people's lives. Where do we learn how to become self-reliant, self-sufficient, and resourceful? We should learn these life-supporting attributes from our parents. The political liberal left will tell us that the homeless are victims of a non-compassionate Republican economic policy, but this is just another Democrat lie. Research study has proven that over 90 percent of homeless people have severe mental disorders or chronic substance abuse problems.

It has also been proven that children with two supportive parents have a less percentage of non-genetic mental disability and substance abuse problems. The government can no longer afford the treatment facilities to house these people as they did in past decades, so they end up living on the street. In Atlanta, we have a very large Asian, Latino, African, Indian, Middle-East, Caribbean, and Jewish population. It is some strange coincidence that I see none of these groups represented in this city's homeless population.

Someone historically famous once said, "If you give a man a fish, he will eat for a day, but if you teach him how to fish, he will eat for a lifetime." That is what good parents do.

Further documenting Atlanta's decline is the story of a gentleman who owned a complex of town home apartments. He wanted to rent to married couples or married families only, but local discrimination laws prevented him from doing so. He preferred to rent this way for the obvious reason that, statistically speaking, married people make better tenants—they are usually more conscientious about property maintenance and the paying and maintaining of lease agreements because they usually have more long-term investment goals.

As far as I'm concerned, this man's entrepreneurial ambition was unfairly punished by an unjust and politically correct law. After all, there are some property owners who are allowed to rent to single people only, and they receive no opposition for doing so.

All this talk about the victim mentality leads me to the welfare system, which unfortunately is alive and well today. A few minor changes and upgrades have occurred, but the result is still the same— to provide single women with a subtle incentive to have babies without husbands in order to receive more government entitlement benefits. These benefits may be less in actual cash payouts than in the past and less overt about encouraging the male to be absent, but the payoff is still available, just in a different form.

Allow me to briefly recap: In the 1990s, the Republican congress forced President Bill Clinton to repair the corrupt, out-of-control welfare system. Recipients were no longer allowed to receive unlimited monthly checks for years into the next generation of unwed mothers. These monthly payouts became time limited and expired if the recipient could not prove that employment was being pursued.

Sounds good, but at the same time, free child medical care, free daycare, free school lunch programs, and free food coupon vouchers were made more accessible to single women. Soon, the physical appearance of the paper food coupons known as food stamps became embarrassing and politically incorrect. Consequently, those paper vouchers were replaced with a plastic credit/debit card so as not to offend anyone's self-esteem at the grocery store checkout line.

The fact is that the embarrassing physical appearance of food coupons was part of the deterrent to becoming too comfortable receiving them. The original purpose of these vouchers was temporary aid for people who really needed help. People who really need help will work harder to improve their own situation so they won't experience the humiliation of accepting unattractive paper handouts any longer than they have to.

As far as I'm concerned, an attractive credit/debit card simply gives welfare recipients an added incentive to maintain free handouts by birthing more fatherless children. Notably, government food voucher payouts have increased about 17 percent since 2008, and I believe the situation I just described is a large part of the cause. The food stamp credit card also makes it easier to redeem the card for cash. For example, some gambling casinos have ATM machines that are specifically designed to accept food stamp cards in exchange for cash. It shouldn't surprise anyone to learn that the bulk of that cash is gambled away at the casino rather than spent on food.

At the same time, 60 percent of public school children receive free breakfast or lunch at the subsidized cost of the other 40 percent of parents who responsibly feed their own children. In some Atlanta schools, as many as 75 percent of children receive free lunch.

There is no way to convince me that 60 to 75 percent of parents cannot feed their own children breakfast. How is it charitable or fair for the federal government to force me to feed my neighbor's child when I am a blue-collar hourly wage earner myself?

Since I'm a black man living in a black community, I feel sad, angry, and frustrated at what I see around me. At my place of employment, many of the black women have never been married but have children. I also have other black coworkers who are married, but have grandchildren by their single daughters. Many of them complain about the economic struggle and behavior problems they experience with their children, but they don't seem to understand why these problems exist. By contrast, all the white women I work with that have children are married, divorced, or lesbian.

This point brings me to another alarming counter-culture development I have noticed in recent years. That is the growing numbers of lesbian couples with children, male children to be specific. This phenomenon is one that I have recently seen increase in the past fifteen years or so. I don't know if there is any behavioral science research being done in this area, but I have noticed some disturbing results based on the cases I have personally observed. Ironically, this new alternative family trend seems to produce young males who are more aggressive, narcissistic, and misogynistic than males raised by single women.

When I go to businesses and stores in my neighborhood and see all these single black women with children, I sometimes think to myself, *Is that kid going to rob me or kill me in a few years?* That may sound harsh, but it's a statistical fact that the single mother lifestyle increases crime and poverty in the black community.

Likewise, when my children were small and my wife and I went to school PTA meetings, I would look around the room full of people and realize that 80 percent of them were single women. This has a strong negative effect on education in the black community because another statistical fact is that the biggest reason black children score lower on standardized tests than other groups is that they have less parental involvement in their education.

Case in point, one of my daughters came home from school one day and told me her male teacher had asked the class how many students had both parents at home. After my shock abated that her teacher had enough nerve to ask such a politically incorrect question, she told me that only three kids—one other girl, one boy, and herself—had raised their hands. She then told me her teacher said it was a strange coincidence that the students who raised their hands always completed their assignments on time, consistently had the best grades, and never needed scolding about their conduct.

Even though I've grown used to this type of situation, I was still surprised that in a class of twenty-seven students, only three lived with both parents. My daughter also told me of another teacher in a class that lasts about ninety minutes that is typically broken up this way: the teacher spent the first twenty minutes talking about how evil President Bush's administration was, the second twenty or twenty-five minutes talking about how cute and smart her grandsons are that her single daughter is raising, and the remaining class time actually teaching. I ask, why do situations like this seem to be the norm and not the exception, and why are such teachers protected? I used these examples to illustrate the overall situation and its negative philosophical and residual effect on me, my family, and my community.

In response to the cultural disaster all around me, I took severe steps when my oldest daughter reached what she thought was an appropriate dating age at about sixteen. This was an opportunity I had no choice but to seize with both hands. First, I told my daughter I thought she was too young to date. I told her there are only two real purposes for dating: one is sex, and the other is to find a wife, and neither of these was acceptable options for her at this time. Nonetheless, I told her that if she could meet certain conditions, I would consider it. First, the boy must be neatly dressed and groomed. This meant no baggy pants below his butt and a short neatly groomed haircut is required. Second, they must wear no earrings because to me they give an appearance of androgyny and are less masculine.

After she heard my second condition, my daughter protested, "But, Daddy, the only boys that meet your physical requirements and description are all nerds, geeks, or gay."

After my amusement subsided, I told her I must be able to call the boy's father, who was married to the boy's mother, at their home to discuss the matter. I must have a man-to-man conversation with someone, and I refused to discuss the subject with anyone's baby mama. Fourth, I must drive the couple to the date site and come back later to pick them up.

As I knew all too well, my daughter couldn't find a boy to meet these conditions, so the dating issue died a quick, painless death. When she became a high school senior, I told her it would be okay if she wanted a date for the senior prom, but she decided she would rather go stag with one of her girlfriends, which was perfectly fine with me.

My oldest daughter, Terri, also sometimes reminds me of a Valentine's Day father/daughter dance I took her to at school when she was in the fifth grade. At that time, I did not fully understand how important this one event was to my daughter, even though my wife explained it to me. I just went along with it because I could see how much my daughter wanted me to participate. I remember how happy and excited she was and also how unfortunate it was that I was the only father present at the dance. My daughter also reminds me how the other little girls wanted to dance with me. I later came to realize that this was my daughter's first impression and permanent definition of the male-female dating experience. She also sadly tells me that 85 percent of those young girls who also went on through high school with her are now single mothers.

Both my girls sometimes ask me if I regret not having any sons. I tell them of course not, because God knew what I was supposed to have, but I do think girls are more difficult to raise than boys because they require more emotional support and more expensive maintenance with their clothing and hairstyles. You also have to constantly worry more about their safety, but if you do it correctly, what you get back cannot be measured.

They're not perfect, but my daughters are the two most gorgeous, lovable things my amazing wife has ever given me. I am more proud of them than I can possibly say, and raising them at a time when black culture promotes a victim mentality and makes it hard to find a good black man has given me many nights of poor sleep. My younger daughter, Pia, wrote me the following poem on Father's day when she was thirteen. If the house were burning down, assuming my wife and daughters were safe, this is what I would grab.

Daddy's Girl

I am proud to admit that I'm a daddy's girl, I know I am the center of his life, his world.

I am so much like my daddy, You would think my daddy had me, His lips, his nose, his face, his eyes,

Every part of him is a part of I.

If you hurt him, you would hurt me, Because if it wasn't for him, I wouldn't be. I love you, Daddy, I love you so much,

Your fatherly lectures and your fatherly touch.

We know your pain, we really care, Because if you feel pain, the pain you feel we share. It's okay, Daddy, you're not alone and never will be,

Because me, mommy, and Terri, Arc always here for you, you see . . .

5

Rap Music, Baby Mamas, Bad-Boy Sports Superstars, and Black Entertainers

The rap music that hit the scene in the late 1980s has produced a generation of talented young black men and women. One of the more positive elements of rap is that it has created economic opportunities for these young people. As a result of their successes with rap, many have been able to start other businesses, including their own designer fashion clothing lines, colognes, and even their own music recording companies.

In addition, several positive rap artists have launched successful acting careers as an outgrowth of their music. These include positive role models like Ice Cube, Will Smith, Queen Latifah, and LL Cool J. Lyrics in the song "My Life" by another positive artist and actor known as The Game go like this: "The passion of Christ needed a sequel like I needed my father but he needed the need le. I ain't no preacher but here is my sermon, eat this black music and tell me how it tastes now and [bleep] Jesse Jackson 'cause it ain't about race now."

Unfortunately, many male black rappers seem to possess a gangster mentality reminiscent of the street thug and gun violence present in the early twentieth century in Irish mob and Italian mafia culture.

Though rap has some positive attributes, its negative contribution includes obscene language and misogynistic lyrics, both of which contribute to wayward black culture.

When I look at the evolution of black music, I am frankly astonished. The Motown music generation of the 1960s and 1970s produced young black male musicians whose lyrics compared women with beautiful flowers or breathtaking sunsets. In one song, the thought of a young lady gave one young man the illusion of sunshine on a cloudy day. These lyrics always glamorized women as poetic objects of romantic storytelling.

Indeed, many of the men who lived before music was recorded wrote flattering love poetry that described women as mysterious and angelic graceful beings. They wrote sonnets that inspired men to praise and worship women and protect them as they would rare jewels. What has happened in society and in black culture to make young men alter their essential definition of womanhood?

Today's rap lyrics refer to women as "bitches," "freaks," "hoes," or even worse, as "my baby mama," as opposed to "my wife," "the mother of my children." A popular TV music reality show castoff even recorded in one of her songs, "It's a badge of honah to be a baby mama." On the contrary, that line should read,

"It is not a badge of honor to be a baby mama"

"It is a badge of disgrace to look into the eyes of your fatherless baby's face."

Contrary to popular belief, it does not take a village to raise a child; it only takes two responsible parents. It's like the character Shug Avery said in the movie *The Color Purple*: "I ain't never seen a child turn out right that didn't have a man around, all churen gots to have a pa."

Of course, this unwed mother business in the black community not only causes art to imitate life with its "my baby mama, my baby daddy" references in black music and black movies, it also penetrates our celebrity popular culture, both black and white.

One of our most famous Caucasian female pop music stars has a teenage sister who is a popular TV actress. This unmarried sixteen-year old celebrity recently became pregnant. What alarms me is that the only person who stepped to the defense and support of this young woman happens in most predictable fashion to be one of our popular black female celebrities. I heard no white people speaking in defense of this teenage girl's actions.

How shamefully ironic and sad that the only time I see a black woman rush to the rescue of a white woman is when the white woman cooperates by imitating the new black popular culture of unwed breeding. Here we have a popular celebrity sending the message to black American youth that encourages teenage sexual promiscuity. Insult is added to injury by having this situation exploited on the stage of our primetime nightly celebrity news tabloid TV shows.

When Republican vice-presidential nominee Sarah Palin's unmarried daughter had a baby, I don't recall anyone rushing to her defense, and I in no way intend to imply that she deserves defending. I only wish to point out the double standard. These examples make it easier to legitimize and normalize the illegitimate act of unmarried births and also make it more difficult for whites to criticize blacks in this situation without being accused of racial motivations.

I recall from many years ago that the 80 percent black female jury in the O. J. Simpson trial failed to consider this same degree of compassion, mercy, or support for Nicole Simpson when they acquitted her murderer. Perhaps these black jurors resented Nicole for being a married mother as opposed to an unwed one. Maybe if Nicole had been O. J.'s baby mama instead of his wife, the prosecuting attorneys might have gotten a conviction verdict.

Entertainment culture in American society has definitely come full circle when a movie about white people is titled *Baby Mama*. After all, this phrase originated as a colloquialism in the black community. In one scene in this movie, a white male and a white female enthusiastically exclaim that you don't have to be married to have babies anymore. The very existence of this type of movie is a comedic yet sad example of the new stereotype that we black people have created about ourselves, and the terrible language in today's rap lyrics is likewise a direct result of this behavior.

The fact is, the majority of today's young black males grew up watching their unwed mothers exchange multiple male partners and therefore do not respect women. How can they? The women who raised them do not respect themselves. One way young males define womanhood is by observing the behavior of their mothers.

Of course, young males also learn respect for women by observing their married monogamous fathers' behavior toward their mothers. But if a young man grows up in a brothel, raised by his mother who is one of the working prostitutes, then his reality is that all women are whores. Even when he meets young women who are innocent and virtuous, he has no respect for them because they ail must be prostitutes just like the ones he grew up with.

If this same young male grows up in a home with his married monogamous mother who shows him the image of a woman who is pure and chaste, then his concept of womanhood is that all women, even whores, should be treated with respect.

To put it succinctly, American women have decreased the value of their own potential by flooding and oversupplying the market with their sexual availability. For hundreds of years, male behavior toward women was largely determined by the level of behavior women would tolerate. Today, the available female population is larger than the available males, resulting in a female population of too many who are too willing, which in turn has lowered the standard of male behavior necessary to acquire female companionship. Women's standards have decreased, and male behavior has deteriorated accordingly.

Not surprisingly, two of hip-hop's most talented artists of the 1990s died violently as very young men. Their names were Tupac Shakur and Biggie Smalls, aka the Notorious BIG, whose birth name was Christopher George Wallace. These two extremely talented young men both died in their mid-twenties by similar circumstances.

Tupac was an amazing musician and actor who starred in several movies and was a genius in his own right. Unfortunately, like so many young black men, his talents were not focused properly because he was raised by a drug-dependent single mother.

Christopher Wallace, an intelligent and talented young man, was also raised fatherless. In the documentary *Tupac's Resurrection*, he said the following: "It takes a man to show a boy how to be a man. My mother couldn't show me where my manhood was. A woman ain't reassure you the way a man can, a woman can't teach you confidence the way a man can, a woman can't calm you down like a man can."

If these two young men had been blessed with good male role models early in their lives, maybe they wouldn't have steered toward the gangster lifestyle side of rap music. In gang culture, young males and females who have no paternal family support become involved with a gang. This gang becomes their family, and they rely on the camaraderie and protection of fellow gang members to keep them safe from rival gangs.

Tupac and Biggie's murderers were never captured, but it was speculated their deaths were the result of hip-hop's East Coast versus West Coast gangster rivalry. Supposedly, they were assassinated in drive-by fashion because of some revenge contract hit. A similar fate befell a member of the legendary rap group Run DMC some years ago too. This part of hip-hop culture simply doesn't care if you're a famous celebrity millionaire or not, which is why it can be as dangerous as common street violence.

On the flip side, a lot of hip-hop music is very inspirational and motivating. Hip-hop is one of the modern black man's most poetic expressions of art in music. This is why I would never suggest that anyone stop listening to or buying rap music and why I have always allowed my kids to listen to hip-hop. They love it just as all kids do, but my kids have two parents who have also taught them to appreciate the beauty of Johann Sebastian Strauss, Mozart, Frederic Chopin, and Johann Bach, and they love this music of the classics as well.

My point is to enjoy rap with a balanced perspective. The problem comes in when young boys are unsupervised by irresponsible parents or single mothers. This is when the glorification of vulgar language, violence, sex, and drugs become detrimental to black culture.

I'm also very concerned about the bad-boy black sports superstars who contribute to negative black culture. Too many of them have discipline issues or problems with the law. Not surprisingly, these individuals tend to come from dysfunctional families, which mean they have little or no relationship with their fathers. A very small percentage of young men have the talent and privilege to participate in the most popular sport in America, which is pro-football. This gives them the opportunity to become positive examples to young boys in ways others cannot.

The reason football is America's favorite sport is because in its unique way, it is a team sport that has just the right amount of brutality, yet it is also a noble game of rules, fair play, and sportsmanship. It is a game in which gentlemen and athletes are required to conduct themselves in a proper manner on the field of honor. When played correctly, it becomes a ballet in a clash of will and a test of strength that partakes in elegance, courage, and discipline.

In this very same game of professional football, there are two sets of brothers: one Caucasian and the other negro, which is why they invite comparison. All four men are quarterbacks, which is the most challenging and difficult position to learn and play. It not only requires supreme athletic ability but also discipline, strong leadership, quick decision-making, and fast deductive reasoning abilities, which are all attributes that boys learn from men.

One set of brothers recently made sports history by becoming the first brothers in the NFL to each win Super Bowl professional championship title awards. The Manning brothers, Peyton and Eli, are both excellent role models, both are married, and both were raised by their married parents. Their father was the great Archie Manning, an NFL quarterback in the 1970s.

The other two quarterback brothers had little or no such parental guidance or pedigree. Michael and Marcus Vick both had superior athletic ability, but their decision-making IQ was extremely low.

Michael was an NFL pro quarterback but over a period of several years participated in several incidents of unethical behavior. His last incident involved committing a felony of reconstitute violation that included illegal gambling, racketeering, breaking income tax laws, parole violation, and lying to a federal jury. He had to serve a twenty-month prison sentence. In spite of his great potential, his younger brother Marcus never made it to the NFL because of the criminal behavior he committed while still in college.

The same contrast in comparison can be made with the Williams sisters of professional tennis. Throughout their professional athletic careers, Venus and Serena Williams have usually comported themselves as first-class tennis champions and good role models for all young women to emulate. They became this way because of the hundreds or maybe even thousands of hours spent learning to play tennis together with their mother and father.

Another black professional athlete with a history of strange, immature, controversial behavior is pro football wide receiver Terrell Owens, or TO. I don't think he's ever been involved in illegal activity, but his latest serious incident occurred some years ago when he supposedly made an attention-seeking suicide attempt by taking too many prescription drugs.

Another professional football star, Ray Louis, was involved some years ago in a murder case and was arrested for withholding evidence and obstruction of justice. To Ray's credit, however, he has managed to clean up his life and stay out of trouble since that time.

Denis Northcut, a pro football player for the Jacksonville Jaguars, was questioned by law authorities for paying his crew to beat up his pregnant girlfriend.

Basketball superstar Lattrelle Spreewell likewise has a history of bad behavior, including punching and choking his coach during a game some years ago. Super star NFL wide receiver Randy Moss has been fined by the NFL commission several times for misbehaviors such as trying to run down a policewoman with his car.

Adam "Packman" Jones, another pro football player, has been in trouble with the law many times, and the New York Giant's Plaxico Burress chose to exercise his stupidity and his second amendment right to accidentally shoot himself in the leg in a nightclub with a weapon he wasn't licensed to carry. As a result of physical injury and felony weapons charges, he ruined his football career and was sentenced to two years in prison.

Boxer Mike Tyson's career was eventually destroyed by his conviction for rape.

But the most famous of this group of black bad boy/criminal jocks is O. J. Simpson, who was convicted and sentenced to prison for many years on several counts of kidnapping and threats with a deadly weapon.

The point is, these men all come from dysfunctional backgrounds, and all seem to have the same limited mental and emotional development as your average teenage adolescent male. Combining this with their powerful male bodies and millions of dollars in income makes for a very potent, very dangerous combination.

As for this issue concerning that nitwit malcontent Colin Kaepernick, N.F.L Hall of Famer Jim Brown said Kaepernick needs to decide if he wants to be a political social activist or a football player. Protesting police brutality against blacks during a football game, which happens to be Kaepernick's place of employment is not the proper forum or venue. In fact, according to data compiled and monitored by the U.S Bureau of Justice, the C.D.C and the F.B.I crime statistics, more whites are killed by police than blacks while more blacks are murdered every year by other young black men than by police. Why don't these unpatriotic, country hating, ungrateful spoiled millionaire athletes protest that? Why don't they leave this racist America and go to any other country and find out how much money they would get to market their athletic abilities?

Now Nike has chosen to glorify Kaepernick as the new Godfather saint of hate the police and the hate America movement. I think their new campaign slogan goes something like "Believe in something, even if you have to sacrifice everything." Kaepernick is worth over 20 million dollars and now he has a lucrative Nike endorsement deal. What has he sacrificed? Muhammed Ali, MLK, Malcolm X, Abraham Lincoln, and Jesus Christ sacrificed everything. The only football player that I can remember sacrificing everything was Pat Tillman who walked away from his million dollar career and went to war and fought, losing his life defending his country.

Personally, I believe this is just a racist ploy by Nike to exploit Kaepernick's name to encourage poor black people to spend what little they have buying expensive merchandise. In my opinion, Kaepernick has become the embodiment of life imitating art. He is the real life character that Samuel Jackson played in the movie Django as an Uncle Tom sellout doing the master's bidding on the rich white liberal Nike slave plantation. He and Nike are merely phony left wing self-righteous hypocrites. When we as Americans go to a sports event, we are there for pleasure and fun. We want to escape the stress of politics. What has become of this country when we can no longer go to a ball game, a music concert or even now just buy a pair of shoes without having some uneducated liberal fool's politics forced down our throats?

An interesting statistic about criminal behavior is that the demographics of criminality cannot be attributed to any particular racial, gender, or socioeconomic group. Instead, criminal behavior is overwhelmingly associated with marital status. More than 90 percent of violent criminals are unattached single males, which is just another good reason for settling down and establishing an intact family.

Then there's the interesting phenomenon of the steadily decreasing number of black players in professional major league baseball. Though sports pundits, sports journalists, and sports talk shows are willing to discuss the subject, they always avoid the fundamental reason for it: baseball requires the manual dexterity of throwing a spherical object with one hand and catching it with a glove on the other hand as well as making a swinging motion with a wooden bat to cause forced contact with the ball to propel it in the opposite direction. The fact is, this instructional experience of concentration, focus, and recreation is typically transferred to sons from fathers. To put it another way, if there aren't any fathers around to play ball with their sons, there aren't going to be any sons who grow up to become major league baseball players.

This seemingly simple activity both constructs and displays the special, unique value of a relationship between positive male role models and boys and occurs in sports such as golf and tennis too. Although other socioeconomic factors affect low-minority participation in these sports, with fewer black fathers to participate with their boys in recreational bonding, pro baseball will increasingly be dominated by whites and Latinos.

Of course, the unwed birthrate is also rising for Latinos, but in that culture, baseball and soccer are learned in participation with peers. This is why Latinos in the United States dominate baseball and soccer and black males dominate professional basketball, football, and boxing. These sports only require the development of superior athletic prowess among equals and little to no alpha male instruction.

Finally, I'm also dismayed by the many famous black celebrities who are amazingly talented but are poor role models for black youth. Just look at Eddie Murphy. He may be smart, funny, and successful, but his decision to divorce his wife sets a poor example for his children.

Whitney Houston was obviously an amazing talent, but she was a poor role model for young black women. Her drug use and choice in a marriage partner merely provide examples to avoid. Her reckless ex-husband Bobby Brown, the father of several illegitimate children.

Then there's Fantasia, the young woman who expressed her pride in having a fatherless child while she was a sexually active teenager. She is definitely not someone young black females should emulate.

The boxing celebrity Evander Holyfield is also a bad role model because of his hypocrisy, which I think is one of the more inexcusable offences in life. He may not be a minister, but he has publicly bragged about his Christian beliefs while simultaneously fathering nine illegitimate children by nine different women.

Musician R. Kelly was charged with statutory rape after having sex with fourteen-year-old girls. In spite of this, he was given a positive role model image award by the NAACP, which I consider disgraceful. Maybe Mr. Kelly does deserve a Grammy for his great musical genius, but being acquitted of statutory rape charges does not earn him a place to be honored by what was once a noble and righteous organization. This is a disgrace and dishonor to the memory of the good people who founded this organization, and it forces me to ask myself, what kind of fathers did these young girls have, and what kind of father did R. Kelly have that resulted in such a debased level of debauchery?

This topic also invites curiosity about the numbers of young women who are involved in prostitution, pornography, strip clubs, and other various forms of the sex trade business or what is commonly referred to as the adult entertainment industry. Research indicates that large numbers of these young women become introduced to this and other related lifestyles as teenage runaways. These young women often leave home at young ages because their home situation is intolerable, and most of them have an unhealthy relationship with their male parent. As Chris Rock so aptly put it, "If you are a father whose daughter ends up dancing with that pole, you [bleeped] up; she didn't get enough hugs."

In my opinion, the very worst example of a role model for black people is the Reverend Jesse Jackson, and I use the title *reverend* lightly. What could be more disgraceful, disgusting, and hypocritical than a so-called married minister of the Christian church fathering a child out of wedlock? During the presidential campaign, Mr. Jackson also made some extremely juvenile, low-class, uncalled-for castration references and unfair criticisms of Barack Obama. Jackson seems to enjoy the materialistic fame of his celebrity status more than living the righteous example of a minister.

Of course a discussion of celebrity role models would be incomplete without acknowledging the greatest musical talent in show business history, the late great Michael Jackson. It is beyond amazing that this man died at age fifty yet over a period of forty years created the most incredible encyclopedic library of music in entertainment history. Through his phenomenal talent, he interpreted his music using his own invention of expressive dance moves that sometimes appeared to contradict the laws of physics.

During the first half of his career, he projected an attractive visage that should have remained wholesome. However, you cannot have a complete and honest discussion about this complicated and troubled musical genius without talking about both sides of him. He leaves behind two legacies. One is his enormous astonishing talent, and the other is his freakish weird behavior. During the second half of his career, he chose to damage the best part of his legacy with his inappropriate private associations and behavior with young boys.

He also left behind three parentless children who might not have a normal life; only time will tell. I believe this in part is what Shakespeare meant when he wrote (from *The Merchant of Venice*), "The quality of mercy is not strained, it dropeth as the gentle rain from heaven."

Fortunately, many good black role models do exist, but children need role models inside their home. This positive influence should not only come from someone else just because they are famous. This is where strong present fathers come in, and you can't have an absent father unless an irresponsible single woman chooses to mate with a weak, lazy, irresponsible male, and I use the word *male*, not man, deliberately.

There is a lie compounded by those who say that poverty and bad economic times influence the increase in crime activity. During the Great Depression of the 1930s, thousands of people were homeless and the jobless rate was two or three times higher than it is now, yet the crime rate was very low.

This philosophy is similar to the one that attempts to explain why terrorists are usually young Muslim males. The general lie is that this situation is caused by these young men growing up in underdeveloped Arab countries where the poverty is great and there are no educational opportunities. The fact is that many of the 9/11 high-jackers were well-educated, some of them in the United States, as was the greatest terrorist in history, Osama Bin Laden. Not only was he well educated, he was also a billionaire. A person's morality and behavior is determined by what is inside them, no matter their economic situation.

I've also admired Oprah Winfrey for many years, even though I disagree with her politics. She has created educational and economic opportunities for thousands of people, she's been a good role model for black and white women both, and her philanthropic works are immeasurable.

I'm a huge fan of many other black celebrities as well, but 99 percent of them follow the same monolithic, liberal political views that contribute to the decline of the black community. For example, I enjoy Chris Rock because he is an amazing comedic talent, but I do not agree with his politics, even though his conservative side comes through in some of his standup comedy routines and TV shows when he jokes about taxes or the importance of fathers in black homes.

He obviously believes in the value of fatherhood and its traditional role and importance for children, but he uses comedy to spread that message without being confrontational, and for this I admire him. More black entertainers and celebrities should try to live by this example.

Two of my favorite black celebrities were conservatives Ray Charles and James Brown. Although they both struggled with personal demons, Ray Charles performed at the 1988 Republican National Convention when George Bush Sr. ran for president, and James Brown was the only black entertainer to go to Vietnam and entertain the soldiers during that war. All other black celebrities refused to go as an effort to protest the war, but James Brown, in conjunction with the pleading of President Richard Nixon, volunteered to go. James tried to convince other black entertainers that this was not about politics but about supporting our soldiers and our country. He tried to convince them that it was embarrassing and demoralizing to the many black soldiers there not to have any black entertainers come lend their support. He also spoke to a large black audience in 1968 to try to stop the race riots after Dr. Martin King was killed. For this act, he was commended by President Lyndon Johnson because of the many lives he probably saved from the violence of the race riots.

Frankly, this is why I like conservatives—they're not perfect, but more often than liberals, they seem to put loyalty to the country and doing the right thing above selfish political ideology. If conservatism was good enough for the man known as Soul Brother Number One and the Godfather of Soul, then it's good enough for me.

The bottom line is the good black role models that exist are no match for rap music that denigrates women, the high numbers and near worship of baby mamas, bad-boy black jocks, and black entertainers whose lifestyles glorify bad behavior. Black American culture continues to decline, and as I consistently maintain throughout this book, it's up to black people to solve this pervasive and ever-growing problem.

6

Slavery 2.0

As I stated in this book's introduction, when my people first came to this country, our pedigree was stolen from us and left behind in Africa. Post-1863, when four million slaves were freed, another atrocious practice began to occur. At the end of the nineteenth century, local and state legislations in the south concocted obscure vagrancy laws that were capriciously enforced by local police to exclusively entrap vast numbers of black men who had been reduced to lives of petty crimes because they were descendants of unemployed freed slaves. This was very convenient because vagrancy is a crime based on one's inability to prove that he or she is employed. During this time of post-reconstruction, pre-American industrial revolution, there were tens of thousands of unemployed black men, and once these men were incarcerated, they were then sold and leased to mining and railroad companies, lumber camps, quarries, farms, and factories for their cheap labor. This practice continued until around the beginning of World War II when blacks began to exercise other options in a segregated military.

One of the early documented examples of this practice of convict leasing occurred in 1903 when a black woman named Carrie Kinsey from Bainbridge, Georgia, wrote a letter to President Teddy Roosevelt, saying her fourteen-year-old brother, James Robinson, had been abducted and sold to a plantation. Today her letter still lies in the National Archives of the Department of Justice. The Emancipation

Proclamation was established under the Thirteenth Amendment to the US Constitution, which abolished slavery in 1863. President Lincoln's original signing of the document in late 1862 only allowed for the participation of colored soldiers in the Union Army. The Emancipation did not fully become officially implemented until the summer of 1865 when the Civil War came to an end. That is how the legislative process worked then and still works now. It is deliberate and gradual. We were 100 percent legally freed, but we were still not 100 percent free until over a century later.

Years after the abolition of slavery, a new environment in which the capture of black men or even black boys was seen as neither criminal or unusual had resurfaced. Millions of black Americans lived in that shadow as forced workers or with their family members in fear of the systems whim. Instead of real criminals that were pulled into the system over decades, the records show the capture and imprisonment of thousands of random impoverished citizens, usually under the emptiest accusations of probable cause or judicial process. Instead of evidence showing a true black crime wave, the original records of county jails showed thousands of arrests for insignificant charges specifically written to intimidate blacks, such as changing jobs without permission, vagrancy, riding freight trains without a ticket, engaging in sexual activity, or talking to white women, an offense commonly referred to as "reckless eye ballin'."

An odd coincidence began to transpire: Rise in arrests started to resemble the rise and decline in the need for free labor. Camps began to emerge and spread throughout the south, run by state and local governments, large companies, small businesses, and farmers. These expanding slave concentration hubs became a fundamental weapon of subjugation of any black progress in social or economic upward mobility.

By 1900, the South's judicial system had been mostly rearranged to make its priority to coerce black Americans to cooperate with the social traditions and labor demands of whites. Sentences were given by local judges, local mayors, justices of the peace and men, who usually worked for business owners who depended on the forced labor produced by those sentences. Trial records were poorly or rarely kept, and attorneys were never retained to defend blacks. Financial prophets from this new form of slavery flooded the state treasuries of Louisiana, Texas, Florida, Alabama, North and South Carolina, Georgia, and Mississippi by the tens of millions of dollars. These were states where more than 75 percent of the black population of the United States then lived. The same white business owners who built railroads with thousands of slaves and then converted their slave labor for its use in southern mines and factories in the 1850s were also the first to use forced black labor in the 1870s after slavery was abolished.

The South's highly developed system of leasing slaves back and forth between different factories and farmers and the non-monetary trading for the cost of slaves recreated itself as convict leasing in the 1870s and 1880s. The brutality and physical punishment used against these captives in 1910 were the same as those used against salves in 1840. To fully understand how and why this new slave system evolved from the old one, you have to realize the enormous amount of fear southern whites had after they lost the Civil War. In the late 1860s, whites throughout the South found it extremely painful to accept the shame, disgrace, dishonor, and humiliation of the entirety of what was lost. Many southern aristocrats lost their fortunes and many tens of thousands of lives. Thousands of union soldiers remained encamped over the landscape of their towns. There was the spread of mass poverty and hunger. If that wasn't enough to fear, then what about all those former slaves and their large majority populations in southern Alabama, Mississippi, Louisiana, South Carolina, and South Georgia? Would they soon be given the right to vote, take over governments, and maybe even take our white lands? This vision was beyond any nightmare too horrible to contemplate.

During the final days of the war, the US Congress enacted a bureau to help the South's recently freed slaves. This new law gave that agency the authority to divide land seized by the federal government and transfer at least forty acres of this land to freed slaves, black refugees, and black civil war veterans for a period of three years. That is where the reparation rumor of forty acres and a mule originated. Afterward, the law said the former slaves would be allowed to purchase this property in permanent ownership. Democrat President Andrew Johnson rescinded this law a few months later, but southern landowners still feared the possibility of losing their property to former slaves who outnumbered them.

At this point, General William Tecumseh Sherman had already given forty thousand slaves the deed to four hundred thousand acres of South Carolina plantation land in 1865. This legal fight over land continued back and forth through 1868 when hundreds of former slaves filed law suits against white landowners, demanding that former slave masters pay back wages for crops yielded from prior harvest season's work. All total 1,800 lawsuits were filed, and whites responded by burning down the courthouse. During this transition of the old slavery practices to the re-enslavement process, the violence continued with burnings and lynchings by the Democratic Party–founded Ku Klux Klan. The extremely large plantations that once had hundreds of slaves were now becoming deprived financially and intellectually as well. The slaves had become the real experts at mass cotton production on most of these large farms.

Slavery was introduced to the South in the 1600s, so over the next couple of centuries, whites had become dependent on some slaves to oversee hundreds of other slaves in the day-to-day operation of these large farms. This became necessary because the concept of sharecropping had not yet evolved. Without full expertise in running their agricultural enterprise, white farmers were forced to compete with each other for the labor of freed blacks who were now demanding wages for their work. The Bureau that Congress established found it increasingly difficult to enforce a law to secure land for freed slaves, therefore, northern military commanders stationed in the South encouraged blacks to enter into labor contracts with whites. These contracts were intended to be renewed on a yearly basis, but some white plantation owners coerced their former slaves into lifetime contracts to work their farms. These contracts were reminiscent of the old slave laws in which black workers were forbidden to leave the owner's property without written permission and own firearms, ordered to obey all commands and to speak in a subordinate manner, and if any rule is violated, he or she must accept whatever punishment is deemed appropriate.

Those blacks who could not find honest employment wandered from town to town, begging for food and asking for jobs. To get from place to place or locations that advertised work, they stole rides on empty freight cars or what few trains still ran. They gathered at night around campfires in the shadows of train depots and cotton warehouses on the edges of towns. While they were simultaneously trying to avoid the Ku Klux Klan and other growing white supremacy organizations, some of these wondering black men were armed with weapons. This was made possible because of the Republican Party's amendment to the Constitution's right to bare firearms so that freed slaves could have the ability to arm and protect themselves.

The Civil War definitely settled the question of the South's ability to be included as part of the free United States, but post-1865 offered little defined strategy to detoxify the South of its economic and mental addiction to slavery. Because of this, the role of black Americans in American society would not be clear for another century. Within the first few decades after the war, southern whites rejuvenated themselves with a rapacious desire to reestablish dominance over blacks, which revived the most visceral patriotism of the Confederacy. White southerners started a campaign to defy and subvert the new biracial social order imposed on them and mandated by the Thirteenth Amendment to the US Constitution to end slavery. They organized vigilante groups and militias, tried to impair free elections across the southern region, intimidated Northern Union agents, and terrorized black leaders.

We now see the beginnings of the South's effort to prepare itself for perceived inevitability of the demise of this grip on slavery. In 1862, an Alabama engineer named John T. Milner and his business partner convinced the Confederate government to finance the construction of a blast furnace in Jefferson County to produce iron for the war. This plant, built and operated mostly by slaves, marks the beginning of the vast industrial complex that would surround the new city of Birmingham by the end of the century. By the time that furnace was in full operation, the next year Milner and his partner Frank Gilmer had also opened another complex of mines near Helena, Alabama. Within a decade after the war and the emancipation of slaves, the Helena mines were manned entirely by convict forced laborers, which set the early standards for the marauding against freed black Americans.

This newly found system of slavery was a perfect fit for the new industrialized south. Once again, over the next seventy-five years after the war, who knows how many tens of thousands of descendants of slaves were used as forced labor throughout the south in coal mining, iron, and railroad companies. These were no longer just cotton pickers; these were men who had acquired skills that were passed down as blacksmiths, welders, miners, ironworkers, carpenters, and masons. These were marketable skills that these men would never be allowed to use in the free market economy of America as the legal free American citizens that they were. As Alabama and other states continued to lease black convicts and sell its black prisoners in large numbers throughout the last part of the eighteenth century, John Milner became a key player in casting hundreds of prisoners into a hellish coal operation called the Eureka mines and later selling these new slaves in the 1880s to other coal mines and to the Georgia Pacific Railroad Co. Everywhere that Milner worked convict slaves in the late nineteenth century, he and his business associates subjected workers to the most animalistic and atrocious mistreatment reminiscent of antebellum bondage.

During this time, the attitude of southern whites was enthusiastically acceptable to re-subjugate black Americans to solve what they referred to as the Negro problem. After emancipation and during the years of southern reconstruction, the Alabama legislature passed new civil laws to appease white farmers' desire to recapture their former slaves. The specifics of this laws stated that the orphans of freed slaves or the children of blacks were declared victims of inadequate parenting and therefore were to be apprenticed to their former masters. Since the southern economy was in ruins, state officials and county governments had little financial resources, the idea of reclaiming the forced labor of blacks was the most practical means of financing government services. This method also eliminated the cost of building prisons or returning blacks to their rightfully deserved position in a free society. Forcing convicts to work as punishment became legal because the Thirteenth Amendment to the Constitution, which abolished slavery, contained a clause that permitted involuntary servitude as punishment for convicted criminals, even though most of these charges were contrived.

During the 1870s and 1880s, all the southern states followed the lead of Alabama and enacted their own versions of laws that were basically intended to criminalize black life. Although many of these laws were appealed and struck down by the federal government, new statutes of the same restraints on black life soon replaced them. These were laws that legally applied to all citizens, but it was widely understood that these provisions would rarely or never be enforced on whites. By 1870, every southern state except Arkansas and Tennessee had outlawed vagrancy, but the law was so vaguely defined that almost any freed slave that was not under the protection of a white man could by arrested for the crime. An 1865 law required black workers to enter into labor contracts with white farmers at the first of every year or risk being arrested.

In 1871, former Confederate general and official founder of the Ku Klux Klan Nathan Bedford Forrest leased and sold hundreds of black males, some women, and a few white prisoners to Florida and North Carolina. In civilian life, Forrest was a major cotton planter and railroad developer. White Carolinians led by Nathan Forrest and Democrat Wade Hampton violently removed the Republican legislative black government that had been placed by the majority black population in the state of South Carolina in 1877. Once the new white government was installed, the Carolinas joined the state of Tennessee to lease eight hundred prisoners, most of them black men, to Thomas O'Conner and business partner Arthur Colyar of Tennessee Coal, Iron & Railroad Co. Colyar then joined forces with John Milner and the new white government in the majority black cotton growing sections of Alabama. Altogether they continued to enforce made up legal charges and intimidating emancipated black leaders in an effort to further build the industrial south. The money they made from selling convicts was used to pay judges, sheriffs, other low officials, and witnesses who helped convict prisoners.

Subsequently, gangs of Ku Klux Klansmen continued to rape, pillage, plunder, and break up black Republican political meetings across Alabama. Eventually a white raiding party confronted a political meeting of blacks in Hale County. Gunshots were fired that night, and two men were killed, one white and one black. No charges were brought in the killing of the black man, but even though evidence revealed the whites caused the shooting, black Republican leaders R. H. Skinner and Woodville Hardy were charged and convicted of murder. They were sent to the Eureka mines in Alabama in 1877. By this time, the northern states ratified the Fourteenth and Fifteenth amendments to the Constitution in order to strengthen and clarify existing anti-slavery laws. These new amendments were established to guarantee full citizenship and voting rights to all black Americans. When the US Republican lead Congress passed its first Civil Rights Act, the new state legislatures of the south now included large numbers of black Republicans. They passed new mandatory laws that stated black and white children in the southern states be afforded some type of basic education. By 1871, more than 55,000 black children were attending public school in Alabama.

Even though there was some positive progress being advanced politically and socially, by the 1880s, twenty-nine out of sixty-seven counties were leasing their black prisoners in Alabama. This system was too lucrative for state and local officials, sheriffs, judges, and private companies to give up. The numbers of convicts being sold continued to increase across Alabama, northern Florida and Georgia. As convict selling and leasing expanded in these states, the working and living condition of the prisoners became worse. They were packed into single cramped cabins that resembled the slave ships of the Atlantic passage. The buildings had no windows, and they slept in rodent-infested bunks stacked three levels high with straw for mattresses. They were served very little, revolting, filthy, cold food from dirty coal buckets, and at least 150 convicts shared three half-barrel tubs for washing and sanitation with no toilets. There was no ventilation, less than adequate water supply, and sometimes cruel, excessive punishment and zero medical treatment for the sick and deceased. Prisoners died at the rate of about 30 percent a year.

By the time World War II started, the industrial progress of the south elevated millions of whites from poverty into middle-class status. The growing infrastructure of modern plumbing, electricity, and new roads expanded across the southern region. There was also progress for black southerners, but it was much smaller and much slower. Black men began to earn enough to save their meager wages to buy land, small farms, and farming equipment. But blacks were still second-class citizens under Jim Crow laws throughout the middle of the twentieth century. During this time of both progress and stagnation for blacks in America, prominent black leaders and educators became involved in what continued to happen to southern blacks after Lincoln's emancipation of slaves. Black leaders such as Frederick Douglas, Booker T. Washington and W. E. B. Dubois had begun to openly express their disapproval of the situation during the latter nineteenth and early twentieth century. This is how my own hometown of Atlanta played a role in the illegal exploitation of blacks in the southern penal system. Washington and Dubois gave speeches in Atlanta concerning this matter.

One of our most famous white sons of the south, Henry Grady, editor and founder of the *Atlanta Constitution* newspaper, which is now known as the *Atlanta Journal Constitution*, wrote about how southern industrialism would replace agriculture and change the role of blacks in the south in the 1880s. Two of Atlanta's institutional landmarks were named after Henry Grady—Grady Memorial Hospital and Grady High School. In 1903, Georgia federal judge Emory Speer, who was the overseeing judge in the new slavery cases emerging in southern Georgia, delivered the commencement speech to graduates of Atlanta's Emory University. In Judge Speer's commencement address, he expressed in his noble opinion to specifically restore the honored fame of the late great Confederate military commander Robert E. Lee, God rest his evil soul. It was Speer's belief that slavery was not the worst crime in America's history, but just merely a benign anachronism. This may not have been the best time for black people in Atlanta, but as a native-born Georgia boy, I am still proud of my city and my state and I am a very proud black son of the south.

The presidential election in 1912 of Woodrow Wilson, an openly white supremacist Democrat, abruptly brought on an expansion of Jim Crow restrictions on black Americans. After the civil war until then, black officials could still be appointed to government positions such as postmasters, customs officers, and other administrative roles. Washington government hired thousands of black workers within federal buildings who maintained some degree of civil equality with whites. Wilson barely won the election over Republican William Howard Taft and Theodore Roosevelt in a split election. Once Wilson was elected, he reversed the number of black appointees in his own government. He resegregated work spaces, office buildings, and restrooms by race. Finally, and ironically, it took the timing of another war to free blacks from slavery a second time in the south. A few years before World War II, awareness of the new black slavery began to creep into the northern regions. The Department of Justice began to get involved, and charges were being brought against the southern penal system, businessmen, and local government officials for illegally holding prisoners against their will. Sometimes cases were successfully prosecuted and sometimes not, but the word was officially out.

Once Japan attacked Pearl Harbor to thrust America into war, President Franklin D. Roosevelt knew the violence and second-class citizenship perpetrated on black Americans could be used as a propaganda tool by our enemies against the United Sates. How could American citizens continue to be used as slaves when they may be called upon to defend freedom and liberty for foreigners in Europe and Asia. Roosevelt ordered his attorney general, Francis Biddle, to issue a directive to all federal prosecutors. Biddle laid out a series of federal criminal statutes to mandate the prosecution of slavery. He ordered prosecutors and investigators to build cases around the issue of involuntary servitude and slavery. As the war progressed, the Department of Justice aggressively prosecuted several southern companies for using black men as forced labor. Sheriffs who colluded with these companies were brought to trial. In September of 1942, several teams of FBI agents, highway patrolmen, and deputies descended upon remote farms in Texas and throughout the south.

These defendants were prosecuted under the Slavery Kidnapping Act, found guilty, and sentenced to federal prison.

One of the best and most uplifting examples of the culmination to the end of this sad chapter in US history would be Tuskegee Airman, Val Archer. He was sixteen years old when he changed the date of birth on his birth certificate to add three years to his age and then went to an army recruiting office in Chicago. He had already tried to get into the Navy and the Marines but was told to return when he was older. After the Army recruiters accepted his forged birth certificate without question, Archer was processed into the US Army and assigned to the US Army Air Corps 332nd Fighter Group, known as the Tuskegee Airmen. Before 1940, black Americans were not allowed to fly for the military. In 1941, the Tuskegee Airmen became the military's first squadron of black fighter pilots and aircraft personnel. In 1945, Archer was sixteen pretending to be nineteen when he became part of the Tuskegee Airmen and was later assigned to the 100th Fighter Squadron. At that time, the military was still very segregated, but because the Tuskegee Airmen became such an important and respected flying group during World War II, they were integrated as an official part of the US Air force in 1947. When Archer entered the military at age sixteen, he didn't even have a high school diploma.

He credits his twenty-two years in the military for providing him an opportunity to earn a high school diploma, a bachelor's degree, a master's degree, and having completed some doctoral studies in an interdisciplinary social sciences program. In 2016, Archer being one of the few living Tuskegee Airmen, was honored as the grand marshal in a Veterans Day Parade in a community just south of Atlanta.

In 1944, Republican President Harry Truman established a Committee on Civil Rights to increase the powers of the antislavery statute to clearly criminalize involuntary servitude. In 1948, the entire federal criminal code was dramatically rewritten to further clarify those laws. In 1951, Congress passed even more specifically defined statutes making any form of slavery in the United States an indisputable crime. That second phase of slavery that carried over from the nineteenth century into the twentieth century was just an allegorical metaphor for the enslavement that black people are experiencing now in the twenty-first century.

The slavery that is now upon us is even more insidious than it was in the 1700s because now it is self-imposed. First, over the past fifty years, we have voluntarily marched ourselves back to the slave plantation that is owned by democrat politicians. We allow them to exploit our lack of current and historical knowledge by giving us subsidized welfare handouts to buy 95 percent of our votes. They no longer have to use whips and chains to keep us submissive and obedient; they now use the passive-aggressive racism of low expectation to keep us in poverty. So now we blindly follow them over the cliff like brainwashed sycophantic myrmidons. The second and worst way we enslave ourselves is to continue to download babies like roaches outside the traditional family structure and protection of marriage. But this time, a war can't help us get out of this phase of slavery because we are already in a war against each other. We no longer have to fear the white man lynching us with a rope because now we lynch each other with violence, criminality, bullets, and prison.

7

Make Marriage Great Again?

The reason that most of our own romantic fantasies about relationships result in the finality of marriage is because most of society is too pessimistic to think about what happens when the prince and princess try to live happily ever after. There is an old joke that goes "There are three rings in marriage: the engagement ring, the wedding ring, and the suffer-ring." But the serious process means that first you have to meet someone compatible, then work through the personality differences and the family approval dynamic. Those are the aspects that should be discussed. The idea of spending the rest of your life and growing old with the same person sounds boring to many.

Most Americans of every social, economic, or racial background still want to get married. That is even true of the millennials, but they are waiting until they get older. Businesses have invested billions of dollars and hundreds, maybe even thousands, of websites to help them find their true love. Technology professionals have tweaked, fine-tuned, and improved search engines so that people can more accurately find that perfect soul mate. Our modern lifestyle has made getting married much easier than it has ever been before.

Staying happily married is what has become much more difficult. In 2014, a Northwestern University psychology professor spent a year of research examining as much sociological, psychological, economic, and historic data available. He concluded that as of present date, marriage is both the most and least gratifying the institution has ever been. He says that Americans today expect more out of marriage and they can attain greater equality of which there seems to be no previous example for. But they can only achieve this kind of quality if they are willing to give it a lot of mental and emotional energy. And if they can't, their marriage will be less fulfilling to them than a monotonous marriage was to previous generations because they expect so much more.

Marriage used to be something people did because of tradition, obligation, or to produce children. Now that we can use technology to find our mates, the perception is that we can put it off for a later date or until the conditions are to our satisfaction. We expect a more beneficial arrangement. Many of us now believe that this one relationship should supply us with a full menu of gratification, such as intimacy, support, stability, happiness, and sexual excitement. If the relationship cannot live up to these requirements, it's cheaper and quicker than ever before to terminate. Most of us are not sure if any relationships could survive those challenges, nor is it clear anymore if couples even know what they should expect from or in a marriage. Marriage is the most fundamental and intimate of our legal, religious, and social institutions. It is also the one institution that is influenced by the changes in economic, technological, and cultural factors, which in some cases makes being single more appealing.

At the same time, more and more recent data reveals that marriage is better for your safety, your financial situation, and physical health. A Cornell University gerontologist did concentrated research and surveyed one hundred elderly couples and found that the longer they stayed married, the healthier and happier they became. All of them also said that marriage was hard work, but any endeavor, undertaking, or course of action that you enter as a commitment to improve your life for the future is hard work, just as getting an education, starting a business, or launching a career is hard work. Any decisive action that you commit to for the improvement and security of your future requires work. We live in a time when it's more difficult to stay together, and there are fewer requirements to do so. The clever part is to figure out how to stay long enough to receive the benefits.

There are elements that modern marriage offers that were not present in the old-fashioned concept of marriage in the past, such as a spouse who understands who you are, accepts who you are, but also helps you improve and bring out your best self. That's what you do for each other. You learn to understand what the other one wants and then provide and help them achieve any goals they have for their self and the both of you.

During the past several decades, the benefits of marriage have changed and so have the potential problems. As I stated in other chapters, the roles that husbands and wives play in the home are constantly changing. Children are no longer the main reason for marrying, yet young married couples today are expected to raise a family more fervidly than ever before. Technology provides more convenient temptations to cheat on your spouse, but the legal system and our culture offer less punishment for doing so.

Sometimes, the punishment for staying in a marriage is more than the punishment for leaving one. Some people believed that staying with her playboy President Bill and his famous definition of what the word is, is, Hillary Clinton made herself look weak or that marriage is just a fake phony farce. She couldn't leave because it would have crippled both their careers.

When Beyonce released her Lemonade album, which was supposed to be about her angry interpretation on the betrayal of monogamy. Well, since she is supposed to be this super-feminist, one would assume that the marriage might be over, but that was not the case. These days, if you stay in a marriage when there are justified reasons to leave, it is more humiliating to stay according to some marriage counselors. No one has the right to tell Queen Bey to leave or stay, but I guess her options are still open.

According to the Pew Institute for Research and the US Bureau of Labor Statistics, only 50 percent of Americans are married as of 2014 because fewer young people are getting married. In 1960, that number was about 70 percent. The rest of the marital status demographic breaks down as follows. The other 50 percent of those who are not married are never married, separated or divorced, or widowed. All of those numbers have increased since 1960 except the married. If women get married after they turn twenty-six years old, and there are few financial problems, they tend to stay in their first marriage. If a woman is twenty years old or less, she is likely to stay married less than ten years. Since the 1980s, the divorce numbers have been dropping among all age groups except one: older people. Divorce among this group has increased. As of 2014, research shows that the divorce rate among people over fifty has doubled in the past twenty years. There are more men divorced than widowed over age sixty-five. In 1990, only 10 percent of divorced people were over fifty. In 2010, it was 25 percent. Some of those were second and third marriages, which are usually not as stable as the first marriage.

Some researchers have concluded that marriage is attractive to highly educated people because they believe it gives their children more advantages financially and emotionally. A lot of unhappy marriages end in their later years because they waited until the children were grown and out of the home. The assumption is that the strain and pressure of raising children for some people is too much for some marriages. Demographers at the University of California at Santa Barbara find that overall, parents are spending a lot more time at actual hands-on participation with their children. Today, there is a much more concerted effort of child rearing that did not exist decades ago with parents of the same financial resources. This degree of intense parenting is very true of college-educated parents.

Children are not just cleaned and fed; there is a micromanaged fertilization, preparation, and refined parenting style. This more involved parenting is more difficult when both parents work outside the home, more so than thirty years ago. Even though the roles between women and men are more equal than they were some years ago, women still carry more of the burden of childcare. They are sometimes the more stressed of the two, but this makes it easier for them to consider a life without a husband. They have their own income, extended family support, and their own 401K. People who are still in their first marriage by the time they reach their middle forties are composed of the following: 70 percent college graduates,

55 percent white and Asians, about 50 percent Latinos, slightly less than 50 percent blacks, and less than 40 percent high school dropouts. As I earlier stated, the technology of social media has made it much easier to find support outside the marriage. Now, both sexes realize they have a lot more options that make the single life look less risky. Emotionally, divorce might feel like failure, but as of 2010, every state in the country have divorce laws that make it a lot easier to leave the marriage without provocation, accusation, or consent, and it's less expensive and sometimes even friendly.

Marriages that last forever are longer than they used to be because now people live longer after retirement than they used to. For some people, that's too much time to spend with someone else's bad habits. After ten years, you know all their bad habits and have gotten used to them. After twenty-five years, they may have created new ones. Most anthropologists, sociologists, and zoologists concluded that monogamy is not the natural state for most animals, human animals included. The conventional theory is that humans invented monogamy to protect and build societies and families and to reduce aggressive competition among males.

Monogamy also saves humans from the time-consuming exercise of searching for new mates or recovering from past bad relationships. Maybe because fidelity is so difficult to maintain these days, cheating is not the foremost reason for ending a marriage as it used to be. Now, more couples are willing to reconcile if there is an effort of contrition displayed along with the possibility of professional counsel. For those who have the stamina, patience, and discipline to remain committed, data seems to increase, suggesting that a long marriage is worth the plod. Studies indicate that married people are healthier, have better sex lives than singles, and usually die happier.

Most erudites concur that the beneficial health effects are vigorous. People that are happily married are less likely to have heart disease, strokes, or depression, and they cope with stress better and heal faster to potentially debilitative diseases. Most of these positive health benefits usually apply only to happily married people, but a study in May of 2016 found that even a bad marriage was better for diabetic men. Some of these findings could be the result of a prejudicial selection process. Substance abusers and clinically depressed people don't usually attract people that are emotionally healthy; ergo, fewer married people are addicted or depressed. Some of these studies could have to do with something more ordinary, such as married couples are more likely to have healthier habits and behavior because their lives are more routine and other people may depend on them. A scientist at the university of California at Santa Barbara says that all these studies of marriage are not accurate. She says that if you believe a long marriage is healthier than staying single, then you have to compare the people who chose to stay married with the people that chose to stay single. According to her, no such studies have been conducted.

Some researchers claim that married people are healthier only because they usually have more money, share expenses, and can afford better healthcare. Perhaps these couples' better physical condition might not be because of their marriage but because birds of an affluent feather flock together and are more likely to get married in the first place. Even if that is true, it has been proven that married women's financial condition is usually better than divorced women's unless she divorced a rich man. Labor economists at the Urban Institute say that divorced women have the highest poverty rates of all aged women in the United States. But it's not all about money; there's also sexual fulfillment. In 2011, The Kinsey Institute conducted a study of sexual gratification in the United States, Brazil, Japan, Spain, and Germany and concluded that married women were sexually happier after fifteen years than they were in the first fifteen years of marriage.

Marriage researchers and educator John Gottman says that excluding sex, older married couples tend to behave like young married couples. The surprising observation is that the longer couples stay together, the greater sense of tenderness and kindness they feel and express to each other. His research reveals that later in life, your relationship returns to much like it was when you were courting. Then there are rare cases where the marriage comes full circle and you get lucky enough for the relationship to be in a special place. If you get to that place, it is as if you can hear each other's thoughts and finish each other's sentences. It is sort of like the Vulcan Mind Meld for those who are old enough to remember the original *Star Trek* TV show from the 1960s. It is a comfortable, complete, and fun place to be. This is a point where this mystical, ethereal light clicks on in the marriage. However, the biggest factor that ironically discourages feelings toward divorce may be the same as the one that causes divorce: the children. As I stated in other chapters, most sociologists and therapist agree that kids from intact homes, for the most part, do better in most areas of life than kids from divorced homes, unless the marriage is highly dysfunctional. Not all children of divorce are emotional wrecks as adults, but the statistics in this area don't look good.

Research also reveals that as adults, children from divorced homes have a greater chance of being poor, not finishing school, having mental illness, being unhealthy, and getting divorced themselves. So, of course, what would this say for kids whose parents never even bothered to get married in the first place. In the black community, this trend has become a national disgrace. It is true that poverty in itself can be the main contributing factor to all these other calamities of life. However, studies have shown that even children who grow up in low-income family but where the marriage is supportive and stable still rise above it as adults. There are still a great many things that we don't know about the human psyche and what keeps people together. We do know that if people marry after age twenty-six, graduate college, don't get pregnant before that, and have decent jobs, they are likely to stay together. If people date those who have the same background and values, they usually stay married. Also, those who are more religious tend to stay married more than those who are more secular.

According to a Bloomberg article by Siraj-Datoo, married Americans are unhappier than ever. The Baby Boomers are getting divorced at record-breaking numbers, and the numbers of Americans who say they are very happy in their marriages has fallen from 68 percent in the early 1970s to 60% -percent now. The types of people who tend to be happiest with the quality of their marriage are religious people, people with extreme political views (in either direction) and rich men. Datoo further says that the percentage who rate themselves very happy in marriage are, by characteristic: men at 64.6% percent; women, 60 percent; non-religious, 59.2 percent; religious between 59.1 and 66.7 percent; liberal between 58.3 and 65.8 percent; moderate, 60.9 percent; and conservative between 62.1 and 68.5 percent. These numbers are based on General Social Survey data by University of Maryland.

So what's the secret to staying married? It's difficult to do exact scientific testing of what actually makes a marriage last because it's not so easy to conduct experimentation with real peoples' lives and still maintain perfectly scrupulous standards and practice. But over time, sociologists, psychologists, and therapists have observed consistent patterns. One of those patterns is the consistency in avoiding negative forms of communication even if there's an argument. Never allow arguments to go down to a condescending level. Negative communication starts a domino effect that breaks down intimacy. It's normal for couples to have disagreements, but you must keep the comments fair and learn to admit when you are wrong. Remember to always allow yourself to get back to doing the things that you know makes your spouse feel appreciated. Participate in activities together that you both enjoy. Be sure to continue expressing those tender words of affection.

There has always been this unrealistic fantasy about finding one's soul mate, whatever that means. Most of the people who look for and then claim to have found a soul mate, get divorced. The conventional concept of meeting one's soul mate at first sight is a romantic myth. In reality, the soul mate is something that you develop over a period of time. The key is that both partners, not just the woman, should exercise the emotional practice of keeping the love alive. The final piece of advice that most experts give for a long-lasting marriage is to do the practical things in finding a mate. Those are the things you never think about when you are being bombarded and overwhelmed by all the raging hormonal urges and feelings of romance and love. Once you surrender to all those urges and emotions, it becomes too late to make wise and healthy choices. Therapists advise you to conduct your own personal amateur investigation of your potential mate. Is their background similar to yours? How do they feel about children, religion, etc., and then don't ignore any red flags. After all that, pray and cross your fingers. Mark Twain said, "To get the full value of joy, you must have someone to share it with."

8

Black Leadership Past and Present

Unfortunately, black America no longer has leaders like Martin Luther King Jr., Medgar Evers, or Malcolm X. Most present-day black leaders are race pimps who never address the real problem in the black community. White conservative politicians do not mention this silent problem because they fear being demonized as racists. Liberal politicians won't speak on it because they use entitlement bribes to buy votes from the lowest socio-economic segment of the black population.

Even black ministers don't dare speak of the illegitimate birthrate because they fear a 70 percent loss of their church audience, which is the same as losing 70 percent of their pelf revenue. The Reverend Jasper Williams Jr. of Salem Bible Church in Atlanta dared to comment on this very subject at Aretha Franklin's funeral. He was vehemently vilified for doing so. The local media labeled his comments as controversial. If he had been a minister of any other religion making these statements in a Buddhist, Muslim, Hindu or Jewish temple or church about women of those religions, it would probably be accepted. But since he is a black Christian minister speaking on the unhealthy immoral behavior of the black people, he was highly criticized when he should have been complimented and commended. What does this say about black America? Whatever it says, it ain't good. For many, the Christian ministry is a business of capitalistic enterprise first and foremost, which means its financial revenue is more important than revealing biblical truth or laws. Every black minister in every black church in America should have something instructive and critical to say on this subject at every Sunday sermon, but alas, they do not.

One of the more alarming examples of this fact was revealed to me recently when I heard a black Christian minister give a television interview that included the discussion of single mothers. This minister defended single mothers by making the comment that the mother of Jesus was a single mother.

What a stupid and sacrilegious statement. I don't believe a white minister would say something that dumb. Whether Joseph and Mary were officially married or not, there are two very important biblical facts this so-called minister obviously doesn't get. One is that Jesus was raised by his stepfather, and the other is that Jesus's mother was a virgin according to the Christian Bible. She did not become pregnant with Jesus by having sex with Joseph or any other man. She was impregnated by God. God was Mary's only "baby-daddy," and she was God's only "baby-mama."

As I mentioned earlier, a duplicitous attempt in the 1990s by so-called black leaders to make black men accountable to their children and women was called the Million Man March. This noble gesture did not succeed, and our present situation is worse now than it was then. The reason it failed is that the problem was never accurately addressed.

The march merely vocalized problems that were already acknowledged, whereas the solution needed to come from preemptive and proactive prevention. The fact is, the participants of the march put misplaced effort into trying to change the natural and anthropological behavioral urges of the male.

The human male is hard-wired to want to mate with any available willing female he desires. This is a scientific fact of biology that cannot be changed by some racially propagandized march. The type of male who most accurately fits this behavioral profile is the single male with or without children. Therefore, single black men should have been targeted and recruited to attend the march. The single fathers among them should have been encouraged to make an attempt at reconciliation with the mothers of their children and to reunite with the family they helped create and abandoned. If reconciliation was not possible, they should have been encouraged to pledge to spend as much time with their children as possible. Inviting the participation of married men was simply a logistical waste of time and space that could have been used for the transportation and presence of more single men.

Just as Dr. King told us how segregation retarded the national growth of the south, our present fatherless condition in the black community is retarding the national growth of black people by placing many of our people socially, economically, and educationally behind the rest of the nation. Yet within the black community are many people of goodwill whose voices are unheard, whose direction is unclear, and whose courageous actions of destiny are unseen. These millions are now called upon to gird their courage and speak out to offer the leadership that is needed.

History will record that the greatest tragedy of this period of our social decline is the silence of those who understand but remain quiet in support of political correctness. When Dr. King spoke similar words decades ago for a different reason, he did not know they would have such a prophetic double meaning.

Dr. King also told us that one day, history would judge our generation harshly, not only because of the immoral misdeeds of the children of darkness, but because of the callous indifference and apathy of the children of light.

There are people today in the black community besides me who see the real cause of our problems but remain silent. Just like the white people in the 1950s, who hated and disapproved of what they saw but remained silent in fear, the silence of these individuals makes them just as guilty as the actual perpetrators.

Today we have black people who don't like what they are seeing all around them but do not speak out because they fear being demonized for being judgmental. It is not judgmental to express verbal disagreement, disappointment, or disapproval, nor is it judgmental to acknowledge or recognize what is unhealthy. It becomes judgmental only when reward is given or punishment is enforced. Dr. King understood this, but this part of his message is seldom mentioned.

He not only amplified the wrong of racist policies in the US government against its black citizens, he also spoke to black people about the futility of violence, self-indulgent anger, and self-pitying victimization. He also spoke about such things as a neatly groomed physical appearance and the value of education and a person's responsibility and accountability.

These lessons from Dr. King have been lost. We are only told about his famous "I Have a Dream" speech, but there was so much more. His complete message is the total antithesis of what the pretentious black leaders of today offer. Today's black leaders only give us demagoguery for the sake of empty disputation, but time and again, Dr. King reminded us that the ultimate measure of a man cannot be assessed in a time of comfort and convenience. Rather, the true measure of a man is revealed during his time of challenge and controversy.

Dr. King rose to the challenge and controversy when Rosa Parks was arrested for refusing to give up her seat to a white person on a bus. This one strong defiant black woman launched Dr. King and the Civil Rights Movement onto the world stage and inspired him to start the historical bus boycott and his great marches.

> "Rosa Parks remained seated,
> So Dr. Martin Luther King marched,
> Ergo Barack Obama ran..."

With that said, I admit it pains me that so many black people are Democrats. Likewise, it's disappointing that the few good black role models and leaders we do have today tend not to be accepted within the black community because they are conservative.

It's hard for me to understand this. Black conservative author Angela McGlowan, who wrote the book *Bamboozledin*, in which she exposes how the Democratic Party has fooled, hypnotized, and brainwashed blacks for decades. She examines history step by step and determines that Democrats have never done anything to actually help black people. For example, it was the Republican Party that eliminated slavery, gave America the Martin Luther King holiday, and even started the NAACP.

Black conservatives like Michelle Bernard, MS NBC political analyst, try to tell us that what Democrats offer is useless and harmful, but many black Democrats see black Republicans as sellouts, traitors, or Uncle Toms. Welfare, for example, only disassembles the black family by offering incentives to remove black men from the home.

Democrats have likewise given us affirmative action, which only makes competent and qualified blacks look less so because it is assumed they only obtain given positions because they are black.

Whatever it is you think you are getting when you vote Democrat, keep in mind that this vote also means more abortion, misplaced sympathy for black violent criminals, eminent domain civil rights for terrorists, less right to own a weapon, and of course, gay marriage.

Republicans support gay rights because all people deserve civil rights, but marriage itself is not a gay right or a civil right. Marriage is not a right at all, which is why you have to qualify for a license to get married, just like you have to meet the qualifications to obtain a driver's license to drive a car. Driving a car isn't a right, either.

If gay people wish to obtain a legal document to codify some type of union with a partner, this would be fair. Under such a law, they would have the same legal rights as any married couple, but whatever word they choose, it should be separate, detached, and totally different from the word *marriage*.

By the same token, I believe this right can be acquired without compromising the religious sanctity of marriage as a unique institution whereby church and state are joined together to protect and preserve the existence of families. The institution of marriage has been the most important and primary building ingredient for the foundation of human civilization, culture, and history for the past several thousand years. Using marriage as a phony political tool to gain more liberal and gay votes for the Democratic Party would only desecrate the religious half of the institution.

The term "gay marriage" is an oxymoronic term or a contradiction of itself because the definition of the word *marriage* is a legal and religious joining of two people of opposite gender. It is one man and one woman, which equal one husband and one wife. By physical description, only a man can be a husband and only a woman can be a wife. Two men would be two husbands or two women would be two wives, which would be an inaccurate and incorrect physical description of the word *marriage*.

The true and accurate description of a gay marriage would be a lesbian female married to a gay male, and since both parties involved are gay, they would still fit the physical definition of marriage. Once the definition of marriage is changed from its original meaning to include anything different, there would be negative consequences that inevitably create a false agenda along with any change. For example, there are various legal documents that require information about one's marital status, which would become too vague and ambiguous to understand and interpret.

It would also be unfair to limit the new definition to only include same gender partnerships. Any different kinds of combinations of gender, polygamies, or any number of pluralities would have to be included under the same rights or law. Same gender civil unions would be the fairest manner to grant same-sex couples any and all legal rights to a lawful union. This alternative could and should not be denied to them because it would indeed be a violation of their civil rights. This is also an issue that all politicians both liberal and conservative agree on.

This legal method would also expose the phony hypocrisy of the left and gay rights activists who insist on confiscating the word *marriage*. If they are not satisfied with civil union rights, then their agenda is not about freedom.

This would reveal their egotistical and selfish purpose to destroy the meaning and status of the marital institution as a whole. It would prove that their goal is to strip away the identity and appearance of marriage so that it becomes unrecognizable forever. Elton John, the most famous and richest gay man in the world, opposes same-sex marriage. For me, that closes the debate and ends the argument.

If marriage is intended for the procreation of the family, anything different from its present definition undermines the future of the family and that includes the black family.

This point introduces a dissembling dichotomy when you realize that 75 percent of black people overwhelmingly reject gay marriage while about the same numbers of blacks apparently accept unmarried pregnancies. This is a bit of twisted contradiction and hypocrisy because unwed pregnancy threatens the future of the traditional family more than gay marriage does. They are both bad for a healthy society and for the same reasons. It also bothers me that black conservatives like Congressman J. C. Watts and syndicated columnist and actor Joseph C. Phillips try in vain to explain to black people why it is they have less political power than any other group. The fact is, we are the only group that votes 90 percent one way. This cancels out any leverage we have on either side. Democrats know they have our vote no matter what they do, and Republicans know they can't get it no matter what they do. This gives both parties the power and convenience to ignore us.

Jews don't vote this way or Asians or any other group. Latinos, for example, have become a larger minority group in America than blacks, and they vote between 35 percent and 40 percent Republican. This gives them greater political power, which can potentially transfer into more economic power than we have, which also makes them politically smarter than us. Whites, of course, still control most of the political power because they have always divided their votes evenly about 50/50. They have done this from George Washington's time until the present, no matter the color or gender of the candidate.

My fellow black Americans, look at it this way: if 47 percent of your group's vote is on one side of the ticket and the other 53 percent is on the other side, you own 100 percent of your political empowerment. Most of the political power is concentrated in those few percentage points in the middle, and those middle percentage points are what the politicians fight over because those numbers represent the moderate and independent voters. This is a remedial mathematical, political fact that most black people have yet to figure out.

It simply bothers me that when white people look at black people, they usually accurately assume they're looking at a Democrat. This means white people automatically know how the vast majority of black people think based on the color of their skin. Just think how much power we surrender by being that predictable! This should make blacks feel insulted and out raged, but I don't think it does.

On the other hand, blacks have no idea what the political ideology of the average white person is based on average appearance. The only white people you can safely assume are Democrats are the weird-looking ones with green, purple, or orange hair or the ones with strange tattoos on their faces and necks or the ones with grotesque, mutilated metal piercings all over their bodies. White people do a better job than blacks of maintaining their power of mystery and anonymity.

Ultimately, black people who always vote Democratic put themselves in a most unflattering stereotype. If a white person were to say that all black people look, talk, or act alike, blacks would feel angry and call that racist. The fact that most of us vote alike just proves that point. It's the same as if someone said, "The only thing black people are good for is playing basketball, listening to rap music, having babies without being married, and of course voting Democrat."

The truth is, we are diverse in many different areas, and so why are we not diverse when it comes to voting? We are the only group that does not balance our voting power evenly. These are some of the many things black conservatives are trying to teach our people, but sometimes blacks are the only people I know who are proud of their own ignorance.

I maintain that black Republicans and black Conservatives are our true role models and leaders because they lead by trying to educate or "kick some knowledge" as we say in the hood. These are the black leaders our people need to guide us out of our self-imposed darkness and into the twenty-first century. They do not lead by using rhetoric; they lead with the example of the ethical behavior they live. They lead by the example of their educational and professional achievements. This is real and practical black leadership.

We no longer need the type of leadership from the middle of the last century that promised to take us out of the dungeons of white racist America. Those days are gone because the black leaders of that time succeeded in their mission of obtaining freedom, even though some of them had to sacrifice their own lives to do it. True racism simply no longer exists in America. Our legal, political, and social system no longer segregates its public and private facilities, venues, buildings, and businesses based on skin color and ethnicity. We still have bigoted and racist individuals and we always will, but they exist in all ethnicities.

9

The Political Consequence

Politics: The world where power and greed masquerades itself within the façade of compassion and morality. I would be remiss in discussing black leadership as I did in the last chapter if I did not acknowledge the internal conflict I feel at the election of Barack Obama as president of the United States. I wish I could have supported this man, but my conscience will not allow it for many reasons. I have mixed and conflicting feelings about him; he somewhat reminds me of the Manchurian candidate. I feel this way not because he is a Democrat because there are some Democrats whom I admire, like black Conservative Democrat Juan Williams of Fox News and author of the book *Enough*. I did not trust Obama because he is the most extreme quintessence of a left-wing radical Liberal. This bothers me in ways that are difficult to verbalize. My feelings are even more ambiguous when I think about the expression on the face of my ninety-two-year-old grandmother, Ruby Gasaway. She told me how excited she felt to cast her vote for the first black president. This is a woman who was born only fifty-two years after slavery ended, but I had to put this aside and remember what I know about this man.

It saddens and frightens me that the first black president in America's history could also be the one who will do the most damage to this country because of his subversive ideology. If this happens, I fear a black man will never again be trusted with that level of power. Many people seem to be unaware of this, especially black people.

There is only one thing I agree with him on and that is the speech he gave to a group of black people on Father's Day in which he criticized the extremely large numbers of absent fathers in the black community. This of course would be a strong personal issue for him because he was abandoned by his own father.

So far I have only seen him get two things correct, and although I agree with him on this subject, I am suspicious of his greater motive for making this particular speech because I believe his reasons were insincere. I believe this speech was a cynical political ploy to pander support from white, conservative, blue-collar working class members of his political party. The only other thing I have seen him get right is his continued process to fight our war against terrorism. This is a good thing even though he has done damage to our overall military foreign policy in other areas.

Obama is extremely smart and brilliant, but "IQ smart" and "president smart" are two different kinds of smart. I do not think he possessed the necessary judgment and wisdom required to manage the complex American macro-economic/military foreign policy that is needed in a president in these dangerous times.

This type of wisdom and judgment was possessed by presidents like George Washington to get us through the Revolutionary War, by Abraham Lincoln to get us beyond slavery and through the Civil War, and by Franklin Roosevelt to get us through World War II and to integrate the military.

Ronald Reagan used it to get us through the Cold War, the Air Traffic Controller Strike, and to repair our economy and military foreign policy from the failed, disastrous, and feckless presidency of Jimmy Carter.

George W. Bush used this wisdom and judgment to keep our country safe from terrorist attacks for seven years, but because of our mainstream liberal media, he will not get credit for this achievement until he becomes a distant memory of history.

I simply did not see these virtues of ethics, honor, or integrity in Obama, nor do I hear them when he speaks. They have likewise never been witnessed in his lack of accomplishments. I don't think he wanted to be president to help the country or its people. Rather, I think he was in it for the purpose of establishing permanent political power, remaking America in his own image, and the egotistical prestige of commanding the private presidential jet Air Force One, the same character flaws I saw in Al Gore and John Kerry.

I also questioned Obama's judgment because of his association with some extremely corrupt people like his racist pastor who said, "The Bible says goddamn the US of KKK." In the video of this same sermon, the infamous Jeremiah Wright gyrated back and forth to imitate a sex act while in the church pulpit as he described Bill Clinton's actions with Monica Lewinski.

I do not know if Obama's children were present to witness this disgrace, but no doubt someone's children were present in the congregation. Obama was a member of this church for almost two decades, yet he says he didn't know this type of thing was going on. If he didn't know, he should have, because if he didn't know, he is too inept or aloof to notice what is under his very nose. This is not acceptable in a president. If he can be this easily fooled, how difficult would it have been for the enemies of the United States to sneak foreign intelligence under his nose?

The only other alternative is that he really did know what was going on and chose to stay in this church, which makes him a liar. Either way, this is the pastor who married him and his wife and baptized his children. This means his two children have had years of exposure to the hateful racist poison of this pastor's perverted version of religious doctrine. For it to have taken three separate public statements for Obama to disown this man after Reverend Wright's comments became public was disgraceful.

Another corrupt association of Obama's is his friend William Ayers, a homegrown domestic American terrorist who bombed the Pentagon, police stations, and other government buildings. Ayers even hosted the celebration to announce Obama's run for the Senate, and Obama co-chaired several board committees with Ayers. Obama claims his association with Ayers was only casual and coincidental, but investigations reveal this to be a lie and show that their relationship was a longstanding one over a much greater period of time.

During the time Obama spent in Chicago politics and the Illinois Senate, he and Ayers partnered in educational reform programs such as the Annenberg Grant Fund chaired by Ayers. Obama used his power in the Senate to channel close to one hundred million dollars to this program along with the Woods Fund, run by Obama's infamous pastor Jeremiah Wright. These funds were funneled through a separate entity called the External Partners.

This program was also connected with corruption within the United Nations, with its overall goal being to indoctrinate public school students with radical socialist beliefs in public education. This is done by gradually replacing reading, history, and literature with politically correct courses like Cultural Diversity, Self-Esteem Appreciation, Minority Studies, Alternative Lifestyle Tolerance, and Aggression Management.

This type of public education indoctrination produces citizens who are less capable of competing in a free market society. Once these people cannot compete on an equal level, they become more resentful and angry with the system. Society is then filled with socialist, activist malcontents. Not surprisingly, Ayers is also on the board of directors of the largest textbook manufacturing company in the United States.

Obama was also a real estate business partner to Tony Rezcko, who is now in prison for fraud and illegal business transactions, and finally, Obama is a former member and present campaign money contributor to a radical left wing organization called ACORN, which was recently charged by the federal government for its history of voter fraud. The corruption of ACORN in the state of Ohio was exposed by black republican Ken Blackwell, who is the former Ohio Secretary of State.

Obama supporters say these are unfair accusations that label him guilty by association, but I say if you apply for the highest position of power and leadership of the free world, then you are guilty by association if the associations exist.

Another problem I had with President Obama that his supporters think unimportant is the lapel flag pin issue. When asked prior to the election why he wasn't wearing a flag pin, his response should have been something like, "I'm sorry, I forgot it today, but from now on, you will see me wearing it every day because I am grateful and proud to wear the American flag."

That was a no-brainer. Whenever you run for public office, every politician knows that there are four things you do: kiss a baby, throw a baseball, bite a wedge of apple pie, and wave the American flag. This is political science 101, but then Senator Obama flunked again.

The flag pin thing sort of reminds me of those old vampire movies when the people don't know who the real vampire is, but when one of the people accidentally exposes the cross hanging from their neck, the vampire quickly moves away. The person then asks the vampire what's wrong and the vampire gives some phony answer about being allergic to metal jewelry. Obama's excuse was just as phony.

I also think it showed very little class for Obama to play the race card when he made the comment that Republicans were trying to scare voters away from him because he doesn't look like the pictures on the dollar bills. Not only was that statement a lie, it was unbecoming of a future president.

I cannot imagine Condoleezza Rice or Colin Powell making such a statement. If race had been a factor for white people, Obama would never have gotten the nomination, but that doesn't mean it wasn't a big factor with black voters. Obama won the nomination because of the overwhelming support he received in the primaries from white voters in states that have almost no black population, but his nomination for president and the general election are different, with three different elements at play. First is the black vote, second is the white vote, and third is the media.

The black vote was decided based on racial loyalty. Although black people always vote 90 percent Democrat, they voted for Obama about 97 percent. I realize that an isolated number of whites voted against Obama because of his color, but that number was balanced out by the small number of whites who wanted to be the first generation of whites to vote for the first black president.

The remaining 98 percent of white voters cast their ballots for political reasons that were irrelevant to skin color. Obama won the election with about the same number of white votes as did George Bush in 2004, which was about 52 percent to 48 percent in both elections. Obama received more white votes than Bill Clinton, Al Gore, John Kerry, George Bush, and John McCain.

I constantly hear my black friends, coworkers, and family members complain that they noticed a silent anger and disappointment among whites after the election. I unsuccessfully tried to explain that the whites they saw disappointed were unhappy because they're Republicans, not because Obama is black. If Obama were a Republican, those same whites would have been just as giddy, happy, and gloating as much as any black person.

Then there's the media influence. The 90 percent-plus mainstream liberal media consisting of ABC, NBC, CBS, CNN, and most of the newspaper and magazine print media had two vested interests. First, this election was their golden opportunity to finally get a Democrat back in office; and second, it was their first chance to get a black elected.

The only time I saw racism or sexism in this recent election process was when liberal Democrats viciously attacked female and black conservatives. For example, Sarah Palin was repeatedly criticized for running for vice president as the mother of five kids. Those criticisms were never used against John Edwards when he ran for vice president or against any male politician, and Edwards also has small children, a wife who was fighting cancer, and he now has a baby mama on the side.

I also remember the Senate hearings back in January of 2008 when Democratic Senator Barbara Boxer grilled Condoleezza Rice about the war. She said something to the effect that Secretary Rice could not understand the pain of loss that a mother feels when a soldier is killed because she has never had a child. That was a cheap shot, one Rush Limbaugh described as a low blow punch right below the ovaries. I heard no one in the media defend Secretary Rice or Governor Palin against these unfair criticisms, but they defended Obama against false race claims quite frequently.

The same Senator Boxer played the condescending version of the race card against Harry Alfred, president of the National Black

Chamber of Commerce. In another, more recent, Senate hearing, Congresswoman Boxer scolded Chairman Alfred for not supporting Obama's Cap and Trade Bill. She told him that he should support this legislation because other black organizations did.

When Obama went on his celebrity rock star tour of Europe and the Middle East, he also refused to visit the wounded soldiers who were in the hospital there. He made this decision after the Pentagon informed him that he could not bring in cameras for his photo ops, and he only made this trip after the conservative media criticized his foreign policy credentials.

Obama also had his own presidential seal placed on the front of his podium whenever he traveled to a city to make a speaking engagement though he stopped this practice once the conservative media criticized him for it.

When you run for president, you should know how to behave presidentially, which is different from the arrogance of acting like you are the president before you are. Obama clearly did not understand the difference between the two.

I was also disturbed by some of Obama's responses at Saddleback with Rick Warren. When asked when a baby's human rights begin, he said a specific answer to that question was above his pay grade. I find that to be a very vacuous response. If a simple question like that is above his pay grade, how can military or economic questions be within his pay grade? Another interesting question Reverend Warren asked Obama was whether or not evil exists in the world, and if so, how should it be handled? Obama responded by saying that there is evil in the United States and that we have committed evil in our efforts to go after evil.

He refused to bring himself to refer to our enemies as evil, including an enemy that can attach a bomb to a baby and use it to kill those they hate. The only evil he could apparently think of was inside his own country.

I also disagreed with Obama's solutions to repair the economy, including raising taxes on the individuals, businesses, companies, and entities that provide the jobs and economic opportunities for the people this ailing economy is hurting.

President Bush signed a presidential executive order to start the production of oil exploration here in the United States in 2009 for the purpose of lowering gas prices.

President Obama vowed to reverse that order after his inauguration.

His excuse for doing so is to stop man-made global warming. All credible scientists agree that global warming does exist, but it is a cyclical change that the planet experiences every so many centuries. Man-made global warming is a hoax that Democrats use as a political excuse to increase taxation, punish American economic freedoms, and destroy the industrial base of American capitalism.

While watching an ABC weekly news show, one of the commentators and columnists, Donna Brazile, made an interesting comment during the Don Imus controversy. Ms. Brazile is black and an extremely intelligent lady; she is also a very liberal Democrat and an enthusiastic Obama supporter. While she made what I thought were some unfair criticisms about rap music, she also boasted that rap music is not allowed in her home. I think it would have been more impressive if she had said that unmarried pregnancy is unacceptable in her home. This is the kind of constructive message that black conservative leaders try to send our young people.

It bothers me when black people continue to blame rap music for the black community's problems. Illegitimate births cause the problems in the black community and these births also influence whatever problems or negative stereo types you might see in rap music, not the other way around.

I once heard Obama say he teaches his daughters morals and values, but if they make a mistake, he doesn't want them punished with a baby. First of all, you can only become pregnant by having sex, and you cannot have sex by mistake. Sex is an intentional action that you do on purpose. One of my biggest pet peeves is the misuse, excuse, and incorrect definition of the word *mistake*. If I lock my keys inside my car, that's a mistake. Second, I don't think of a baby as a punishment, but if President Obama saw it that way; the lesson to be learned is that sometimes punishment is the correct consequence for promiscuous or immoral behavior.

The megalomaniacal pompous arrogance of this man bothered me in ways I cannot fathom. I have heard him make several scary comments, but the one I remember best gave me the worst bone-chilling fright so far. In one of his speeches, he said, "Americans cannot continue to eat what they want and drive those big SUVs, and keep running their air-conditioning at 70 degrees in summer and their heat at 80 degrees in winter, and expect other countries to agree with it." This was the most tyrannical and fascistic statement that I have ever heard an American president make.

I will agree that my personal lifestyle may not be healthy for me or the ecological environment, but that choice is among the freedoms and pursuit of happiness given to me by God and protected by the constitutional laws established by the founding fathers. Then King Obama has made an authoritarian decree to punish me for, or stop me from, driving the car that I can afford to choose or living in my home at a temperature that comforts me or eating what I choose. I now live under the regime of a president whose concern is not for American citizen's rights.

His concern is that foreign countries disapprove the rights of the US citizen. Now that I might be forced to give up my big SUV, did Master Obama give up his big private air-polluting presidential limo that travels only five miles per gallon of fuel or his private helicopter or his private presidential jet that his wife takes to Paris to shop? If I am forced to give up the foods I like, did President Obama give up his carbon foot printing cigarettes? This type of hypocrisy and double standard are the things that anger me most about liberal democrats.

I also find it disturbing that many black people, with whom I discuss Obama, always seem to make some religious reference to his being elected. I have heard this opinion expressed by members of my hometown local media. I have even seen church marquee billboard signs advertising Sunday sermons about Obama. I have also witnessed similar opinions from the national liberal media as well. Evan Thomas of *Newsweek* magazine literally referred to Obama by actual comparison as God in an interview he gave to MSNBC, or as Rush Limbaugh refers to as MSNBC.

They often sound reminiscent of those people who have recently become members of a new religious cult. It has been reported that during the presidential campaign, Obama's campaign headquarters staff members traveled to different communities throughout the country to make the usual door-to-door visits to solicit votes. During these visits and also phone calls, the campaign staff was instructed not to discuss or ask questions about why voters should support Obama or his policies. They were instructed instead to specifically give or present testimony on how they came to Obama.

This is similar to the technique and language that evangelicals use when they recruit door to door. I also find it curious that this presidential messianic deliverer is the first president in history to reject the celebration of the National Day of Prayer. This is a day celebrated every year on May 7 as a reminder that America was established by people of faith and blessed under Judeo-Christian philosophy. Every president as far back as I can remember has acknowledged this day, but not this guy. My guess is that he did not want to offend his atheist voters, but he obviously does not care if he might offend some voters of religious faith.

He also gave a speech at Georgetown to a religious University. The stage platform from which he spoke had religious symbols on it that would have been visible behind him. Before his speaking engagement took place, he ordered all these religious symbols to be covered with plywood and drapery. I believe he is also the first president to hold no membership at any church. I find it curious and disturbing why so many people, especially black people, place so much religious implication on a man who is obviously the most secular or anti-religion president so far.

During the time when the president was trying to pass legislation to conduct the government seizure of the medical healthcare system, he used a hypocritical religious point to make his case. He said in a speech that it was a moral imperative for the government to provide medical care for everyone because the Bible says, "You are your brother's keeper." The president's income tax data, which is a matter of public record, revealed that he gave less than 4 percent of his millionaire wealth to charity, and most of these were fake charities created by, and in the name of, his wife and his former pastor, Jeremiah Wright. The same charity donation numbers hold true for his vice president, Joe Biden.

Meanwhile, the evil George Bush and Dick Cheney give more than 20 percent of their annual income to the poor. Also President Obama's brother still lives in an African village in a six-foot-by-nine-foot hut with a dirt floor. The president is obviously not the keeper of his own brother.

If Obama's supporters were correct with their religious comparisons, it would indicate that God has changed or reversed two of his most famous rules. One would be about using his name in vain, and the other would be that rule that mentions something about "thou shall not kill." Because Obama's election would mean that he was such a charismatic and persuasive politician that he has convinced God to endorse the most extreme pro-abortion candidate in political history. It saddens and frightens me to see people, especially my own people, use sacrilegious rationalization to justify their own political agenda.

For those who convinced themselves that Obama's victory was divine intervention, they might try to consider the possibility of his victory as intervention from the other side to be fair to God. You should understand that divine intervention can also be used to punish a people for having blind loyalty to a product of the false prophet. In the eighteenth and nineteenth centuries, Southern whites used the same divine purpose argument to justify slavery. They used a perverted religious belief to further their political agenda and to prove that God made blacks inferior to them.

I am also deeply concerned about some of the statements Mrs. Obama made, such as this is the first time she has been proud of this country. For me, that statement is not becoming of a first lady. It sounds like she is only proud of this country because she became the first black queen bee in the White House. I can think of many reasons that I have always been proud of my country. I was proud long before her royal majesty, Mrs. Obama, graced us with her presence. I'm proud because this is the country that liberated Kuwait and Iraq from an evil dictator. I'm proud because this is the country that liberated Germany from the Nazis and stopped Hitler from trying to kill every Jew in Europe.

I'm proud because this country has spread more freedom and fed more starving people around the world than any other country on this planet. I'm proud because this is the country that produced Abraham Lincoln, the black soldiers in the Civil War, and the black fighter pilots in World War II.

This is the country that produced Dr. Martin Luther King Jr., Jackie Robinson, Dr. Benjamin E. Mays, Malcolm X, Hank Aaron, Dr. George Washington Carver, Muhammad Ali, and Joe Louis. This is the country that produced most of the world's great discoverers and inventors because of its free enterprise system and its free market ideas. This is also the country that provided Mrs. Obama and her husband with Ivy League educational opportunities and an extremely affluent lifestyle.

Black conservative author Shelby Steele is one of the greatest thinking minds of our time. His book titled *A Bound Man* offers a truly fascinating analysis of Obama. Likewise, noted black conservative author Wayne Perriman wrote the book *Unfounded Loyalty* in which he exposes a great deal of interesting information, including congressional legislation from many years ago that partnered with the organization Planned Parenthood. This Democrat legislation encouraged federally funded abortions targeted especially toward blacks.

Perriman's more famous book called *The Drama of Obama* mentions some shocking information about the president. In this book, Perriman talks about the original version of Barack Obama's book *Dreams of My Father* in which Obama uses extreme and profane racist language against white people, including pejorative, misogynistic, and vulgar language referring to the genitalia of his former white girlfriend. In addition, in the audio version of the book, he says, "White people's greed starves a world in need." However, it should be no surprise that this version of the book is no longer available. When Obama became senator, he had the book rereleased without the racist inflammatory remarks.

Dr. Jerome Corsey, who happens to be white, is author of the book *Obama Nation*. He was arrested and jailed at gunpoint in

Kenya for writing this book, which exposes even more frightening truths about Obama.

Nevertheless, I expected Obama to win the election for president because the mainstream liberal media decided long ago they wanted an affirmative action appointee as president because he is black, even though he is not qualified for the position. I don't believe Obama was elected president because of race, but I do believe he was nominated to run by his party because of race and a certain percentage of voters voted for him because of race. He would have been elected president no matter what because of the undeserved unpopularity of President Bush, which was surgically orchestrated over the past several years by the media and a majority rule of Democrats in Congress. Again, Obama's nomination was influenced by race among black voters and the media, not white voters. This same factor is true for the general election as well.

The media accomplished their goal by manipulating the dissemination of the information and news coverage of this election. First, they torpedoed Hillary Clinton's campaign because they realized it was more fashionable and attractive to help the Democratic Party elect the first black candidate than the first woman. Race preference is apparently more politically correct than gender preference.

After the media eliminated Hillary in the primaries, they turned their target sites on the Republicans. Mitt Romney was Obama's biggest competitive threat, so they targeted his Mormon religion, but when Obama's religion was questioned, Republicans were charged with racism.

Once Romney was eliminated, McCain became the nominee to defeat. To put it succinctly, the will of the people was usurped by the media, who decided which nominees and candidates would be most conducive to an Obama victory.

One example of media-biased manipulation is how interviews were conducted. When Democrats were interviewed, the questions were simple-minded and sophomoric. When Republicans were interviewed, the questions took on a more aggressive, hostile tone. When Katie Courie of CBS ("Comrade Barack Station") interviewed Condoleezza Rice, the stupid and insulting question was, "Who made you the boss over Iraq?" When she interviewed Hillary, it sounded like two high school girls discussing the cutest boy in class.

When Charlie Gibson of ABC ("Absolute Barack Channel") interviewed Sarah Palin, he used the word *hubris* when referring to her. I have never heard him or any media person use that word or any similar word when referring to a Democrat.

I also recall a report on NBC ("Nefarious Barack Channel") that interviewed some American soldiers in Iraq. Three out of four of the soldiers interviewed said they were voting for Obama because they knew he would bring them home because he cared more about their safety. After being shocked at how cowardly that sounded for an American warrior to say, I remembered that 75 percent of the military voted for Bush twice. Why didn't this interview reflect those numbers?

Likewise, this is the first time in all my years of observing politics that I have seen every single presidential debate moderated by Democrats. This violates every standard of integrity, objectivity, and credibility that exists in journalism. Once I saw this, I knew the media was totally corrupt and in full support of Obama, as are the terrorist organizations Hezbollah and I-lamas, which oppose the state of Israel and came out publicly to endorse Barack Obama's candidacy for president.

This is the equivalent of saying that if Osama Bin Laden were allowed to vote in our presidential election, he would vote for Obama. Why does that not bother Democrats? Why are the people who hate us, the enemies of the United States, so in love with our Democrat politicians? Why do the American media not express any intellectual curiosity about this kind of information? Whoever the terrorist chooses, common sense should automatically push voters in the opposite direction.

With a neophyte president who was a rookie senator with no accomplishments, no experience at ever actually running anything, and a product of corrupt Chicago politics, along with a radical vice president and other Democrat nuts in charge of Congress like slobbery-mouthed Barney Frank, Chris Dodd, Chuck Schumer, Howard Dean, majority leader Harry Reid, and the vapid, insipid Nancy

Pelosi, the worst, most incompetent, most unqualified Speaker of the House in the history of this country.

Once Obama began making extremely unsuccessful policy decisions, his supporters made their predictable phony racism accusations against anyone who criticized his ineptitude. We all had to listen to this for eight long years.

When I look at all the character flaws, poor decisions, and lack of leadership ability, I see the bottom line that brings me back to the overall theme of my message: Barack Obama was raised by his grandparents, but he is still the product of a mother whose husband abandoned her and their child. When I listen to him and observe his behavior, I hear the thoughts and views of an intractable narcissist whose life was strongly influenced by a rebellious, radical, and reckless single female.

During the middle of the Civil War in 1864, President Lincoln said, "Can any government not be too strong to harm the freedoms of its people, yet be strong enough to maintain its own existence in great emergencies?" Obama's despotism of government control is strong enough to destroy the freedoms of the people, which is indeed a great emergency. I hope we are strong enough to maintain our own existence.

Donald Trump's presidency has been plagued with unsubstantiated, unfounded, and unproven accusation of obstruction and collusion from his haters. Yet I remember during the beginning of President Obama's administration, several members of his cabinet selections were cited and or charged with some type of corruption, malfeasance, or tax cheating. I guess that was the hope and change that we were supposed to believe in that he so often spoke of in his beautiful, but lofty and pompous speeches. The truth is that his failed economic policies caused Americans', especially black Americans', paychecks to shrink under higher taxes, black poverty to grow, and our healthcare system to become damaged. His naïve foreign policy made America less respected in the world and less safe from our enemies. Lest we not forget our erstwhile president's biggest accomplishment after eight years, men should marry men, women should marry women, and boys can legally use the girl's bathroom and locker rooms in public schools.

Significantly, Alvita King, a conservative Democrat and author of two books and the niece of Dr. Martin Luther King Jr., has stated that she did not vote for Barack Obama because of his support of gay marriage (which he denied) and because when he was in the Senate, he voted several times to legalize partial-birth abortion.

She is probably the only person in the entire King family who didn't vote for him! Although I continue to believe that Obama is too unqualified and unethical to be president, I do appreciate the fact that his victory is a proven historical example of Dr. King's dream.

But ironically, he was chosen by blacks and the media because of the color of his skin and not the content of his character because the facts about him reveal his character to be inherently flawed. Obama had the reverse Midas touch. Everything he touched turned to feces. If it was something good, he made it bad. If it was bad, instead of fixing it, he made it worse. This is the legacy of the great President Barack Hussein Obama. Thank you so much Mr. President.

As documented by the National Black Republican Association, Dr. Martin Luther King Jr. and his civil rights era followers were Republicans. In the mid-nineteenth century, the Republican Party was originally founded as the anti-slavery party. It was the Democrat party that passed all the Jim Crow segregation laws a century later. Incidentally, those were Democrats who turned those water hoses and dogs loose on black people and overturned school buses full of children in those familiar film footages we have all seen from the Civil Rights protest demonstrations of the 1960s. Within the first year of his presidency, Donald Trump has repaired most of the damage that it took Obama eight years to create. Trump has generated an economic climate that has created millions of jobs, given us a 4-point GDP (gross domestic product) growth, cut taxes and drastically improved our military foreign policy. But Trump's biggest achievement was being the only one on the planet who could put the final nail in the coffin of Hillary Clinton's political career. If she had run against Ted Cruz, Marco Rubio, Jeb Bush or any other republican, she would have beaten them like an African drum in a 1930s Tarzan movie.

This country would have never recovered from Obama, followed by four more years of her parasitic economic policy, destructive foreign policy, and illegal immigration regime. As for me personally, I would have voted for David Duke the Klansman before voting for that rotten to the core, crooked, corrupt, serial lying wicked witch of the Northern Hemisphere and I don't say that because she is a woman. There are at least a dozen women I think are more qualified and more ethical to be president than Hillary Rodham Clinton.

In today's politicized America, conservatives cannot openly express their free speech rights any more. If you wear an Obama hat, a Hillary Clinton T-Shirt, or any kind of democrat bumper sticker on your car, everyone, any and everywhere welcome you. Yet there are hundreds of cases reported of political and verbal reprisal on conservatives when they exercise their God given, constitutional privilege to display Trump signage and republican gear. If you happen to be a famous recognizable conservative in a theatre or a restaurant, the so-called tolerant liberal villagers will use their belligerence to harangue and chase you out with stones, clubs, and pitchforks.

According to Obama's attorney general Eric Holder and that idiot Congresswoman Maxine Waters, violence is the only way to combat conservatives. If that doesn't work, you can always wait until a group of Republicans gather on a baseball field to practice softball, then send a Jihadist Democrat sniper to assassinate as many of them as you can pick off. The liberal celebrities are even more hateful and violent than their mob mentality fans. Madonna, Snoop Dogg, Johnny Depp and Kathy Griffin don't just want President Trump out of office. They seem to want him murdered. It reminds me of ancient times when soldiers of the Roman empire proudly marched and displayed their symbolic Armour while Christians had to whisper their beliefs and hide in silent fear of the Roman blade pressed to their necks.

Republicans founded black colleges and universities and also along with Dr. King pressured Democrat President Johnson to sign the 1964 Civil Rights voting bill. It wasn't until Richard Nixon's Southern Strategy Era that black people changed political parties.

However, I do believe that if Dr. King were still alive, he probably would have put aside any difference of logic and politics and supported Obama for emotional reasons, just as Colin Powell did.

10

Hope for the Future

I believe the best chance to improve the black situation in America is to approach the problem at our first line of defense. Since we cannot change the primal lustful behavior of the male, we must make an appeal to the moral behavior of our women. It is the female gender of any species who decides when, where, and with whom mating will take place. The only exception to this rule of nature is in the case of criminal rape.

Therefore, I'd like to propose the following: an annual million-women march whose agenda is reducing the unwed birthrate in the black community. The only group of women who should be invited or encouraged to attend the march are single black women of child-bearing age. This group of women would be asked to make a vow, pledge, or promise to themselves and their communities to never under any circumstance become pregnant outside of marriage. After all, you simply cannot give birth or raise a child outside of marriage unless unprotected, non-marital sex has occurred.

If all other preventative behavior is disobeyed, then adoption is always the best option. Because of my religious beliefs, abortion is not permissible unless the situation is rape, incest, or to save the mother's life. Many women both married and single are physically capable of bearing children but never do. These women for whatever reasons have made the decision to never by any excuse or circumstance become pregnant. All women have this same option.

We must reeducate our young women to reject politically correct clichés and understand the truth: their chances of future economic success will increase if they raise their children with in a stable marriage. All research reveals that children born to single women occupy the lowest socio-economic position of impoverished and uneducated people.

For example, 80 percent of single women below the age of twenty who give birth will spend at least the next ten years below the poverty level, and most of them will stay at this level for the rest of their lives, while 90 percent of these same young women will never go to college.

The children of these women will likewise have a higher percentage of poor academic performance and are more likely to become involved with substance abuse, premature sex, or criminal activity in their own adolescent and teen years.

We have to recondition our young women so they learn to deny men the ego gratification, freedom, and convenience of conceiving children without the responsibility of commitment. When and if women do this, men who desire children will have to respond by demonstrating more acceptable behavior. Black men who wish to be sexually active will have to make the choice of wearing condoms or become the kind of men who are acceptable as husbands and fathers.

But first, our young black women have to become the kind of women who are desirable as wives. In this way, the million-women march could ultimately empower single black women to improve the outcome of future generations.

Thanks to the hard work and sacrifices of Malcolm X and Dr. Martin Luther King Jr., blacks now have the same rights and freedoms as everyone else, but our present situation is raking us backward to less economic and educational freedom. If we use the same principle those men used, we can solve our problems. If every black politician speaks out, if every black minister speaks out, if every black celebrity with the opportunity to get in front of a microphone or TV camera speaks to this issue, the problem can be solved. Likewise, black publishers and editors of black magazines, newspapers, and the like can spread this message in print to young black women.

This message is for black women to change their behavior and just say no. Black women have to not only be strong independent women but strong independent ladies, because there is a difference. A woman is anyone grown-up and female, but a lady is a woman who lives by a strict moral code of conduct, just as there is a difference between a man and a gentleman.

I am not trying to stop anyone from getting their groove or freak on. I realize that young single people will express their sexual freedoms even if I disagree. I was young and single once myself, but the unwed baby-making has to stop. There is such a thing as discretion and decency, and what happens behind closed doors should remain there.

If you are walking around with children, and it's obvious you've never had a husband, your business is no longer behind closed doors; it is walking with you. The only sexual freedom you've expressed is your right to be a hoe, which is Ebonics for *whore*, and even if it's not true, that is the message you send and the label you wear.

The National Association for the Advancement of Colored People (NAACP) could also be a big help in trying to correct the black fatherless problem. This organization could mandate a new agenda or start some type of national campaign to get back to their original mission. When they were founded, their mission was to advance the civil rights and social opportunities for people of color. Today much of that mission has been accomplished, but we do still have to continue our social, economic, and educational advancement as people of color. This isn't because white people are holding us back; it is because we are holding ourselves back.

Unfortunately, the NAACP has not adapted its mission to fit the new problem. Instead, over the last several decades, it has slid to the dark side and deteriorated into just another radical left wing community activist organization.

Consequently, over the years, many good people both black and white have cancelled their memberships with the NAACP because they see what it has become. This would be a good time for this organization to redeem its soul by using its voice to address the problems and discourage the behavior of unwed mothers in our community. This would get them back to actually advancing opportunities for people of color. They would then truly become the National Association for the Advancement of Colored People, or people of color, the NAAPC.

I'd also like to see public schools specifically address the problem of unwed pregnancies. Since so many liberals want our children to learn sex education, eliminating single mother pregnancies should be the main priority of such courses. If we can teach teenagers how to put condoms on bananas or how to get an abortion without their parent's permission, we should also be allowed to teach them about the immorality, the shame, the poverty, and the societal damage caused by unwed pregnancies.

In many ways, public education is part of the problem, since it is mostly administrated by the left side of government politics and because teachers' unions make it impossible to eliminate or fire incompetent teachers.

This point was very well illustrated in John Stossel's 2007 documentary on ABC called *Stupid in America*. This report exposed "The Rubber Room," the huge office building in every major city across the country that houses all the incompetent, unqualified, and unethical teachers who cannot be fired because of the unions. These teachers just sit at desks in front of computers for eight hours a day and stay on the tax payer payroll.

Another problem is how activist community organization groups indirectly extend their political power and influence to not only educate but to indoctrinate students. Among these are groups like ACORN, which uses financial contributions from lobbyists and other groups to sponsor liberal education reforms.

Some of these reforms encourage teachers to manipulate test score percentages in minority communities by accusing tests of being culturally biased against minority students, while other reforms lower required grade standards altogether.

One example of an education indoctrination practice used here in Georgia happens on the first day of school each year when a teacher sends the children home with a list of required school supplies. When some of the kids return to school with supplies and others without, the teacher collects all the supplies and places them in a large box and redistributes them equally among the students whose parents cannot afford to buy any.

This practice is disguised as a lesson in charity or sharing, but in reality, it is a subliminal socialist indoctrination to teach a child that he or she has no private property rights and, instead, that the federal government has the power and right to confiscate property and redistribute it to whomever they decide needs it more. "From each because of his ability, to each because of his need." This is also an extension of the welfare mentality.

On the contrary, the definition of charity and generosity is that it comes from a voluntary spirit of benevolence, which can only be taught by both parents in the home, not by the government.

This philosophy also teaches people not to identify themselves by their own individuality and talents. Instead, they must identify with a demographic group, whose members are threatened or victimized by some other group that wants to hold them back because of their skin color, gender, or religion. In the end, this practice discourages young minds from exploring their own abilities to acquire what they want or need in life.

Other subversive educational tactics used in minority schools include American history courses taught with textbooks that contain material about mythological afro-centric historical heroes. In these same texts, there is very little mention of people like George Washington or Thomas Jefferson. When such individuals are mentioned, it is only to emphasize that these founding fathers were evil slave traders and slave owners.

Such tactics teach black students an inherent resentment and dislike for their own country, which helps promote the victim mentality I talked about earlier. Some black educators don't seem to realize how important or helpful it would be to black children, or any children, to learn that our second president, John Adams, worked the fields of his own land along with his wife and children because he refused to own slaves.

How helpful it would be to know that ten percent of General George Washington's military were black soldiers who volunteered to fight for this country's freedom and, as a reward for doing so, were granted their own freedom from slavery by General Washington.

In fact, black soldiers fought on the other side of the Revolutionary War too. They were known as the Black Brigades for the British Army and fought against the American Patriots. Would this not be a more positive way to use true American history to illustrate our past and future value of having an allegiance and loyalty to our country?

In other public high schools, students are forced to watch Al Gore's politically propagandized movie about global warming. Also, in some of our universities, Barack Obama's books are required reading by some professors. It would help the black community if we stopped public education from further brainwashing our children into becoming future representatives of the same old black liberal establishment, an establishment that preaches and teaches self-victimization and failure.

However, this is not an indictment on public school teachers. Some amazingly talented, dedicated, and highly educated teachers work in the system. Some of them are members of my own family, but they represent a very small percentage of public education teachers.

My criticism is of the federal government's control and indoctrination of the public educational system as a whole. Our state and local government should have more control of how our public schools are operated. Many urban schools are struggling with the breakdown in enforcing what I consider to be basic standards of discipline. This is damaging because the leadership of any organization drives and influences the culture and that organization. For example, in public schools, if a girl becomes pregnant, she is allowed to continue to come to school throughout her pregnancy. In my opinion, this should not be allowed because it essentially rewards promiscuous sexual conduct. Part of the solution to teenage pregnancy is for the school to enforce a zero-tolerance policy for this behavior. This helps bring back the social stigma of shame and embarrassment for unmarried pregnancy as a whole.

In private schools, students are not allowed to walk around pregnant. If a student becomes pregnant in a private school, she is removed from the school or expelled. Likewise, if unmarried faculty or staff members become pregnant, they are fired to preserve the example and appearance of what is acceptable behavior for the students. In public schools, unmarried pregnant teachers just keep teaching.

I realize that not all parents can afford private school, I included, but all schools should be able to enforce acceptable standards of behavior for teachers and students, not to mention more parental involvement in their children's primary education.

In some public school districts across the country, the alphabet grading system has even been downgraded. In these schools, the lowest letter grade a student can now receive is a D. The letter F has been eliminated and replaced with the letter H for "Held" or I for "Incomplete. F cannot be used any longer because children who fail a course will feel a politically incorrect effect on their self-esteem!

In my humble opinion, learning how to cope with the consequences of failure is part of the educational and developmental process of learning a work ethic. Lowering standards of achievement is damaging to all children, and certainly to children in the black community, but this is just another example of government public education practices that normalize the idea of mediocrity.

A method our new presidential administration will be using to undermine the structure and fabric of the American family is free universal pre-kindergarten for children as young as age three. On the surface this sounds like a good idea because it is supposed to improve the learning ability of children at a younger age, but in reality, it does just the opposite. Just as other government economic programs provide incentives to separate the male parent from the home, this universal pre-K program removes another family member from the home at a younger age, which actually decreases the child's learning ability.

Research shows that the starting school age in certain European and Asian countries is as late as age seven and that these children are smarter, better adjusted, have fewer cases of attention deficit disorders, and fewer behavior problems than children who start school earlier. Indeed, research shows conclusively that it's better for children to spend as many of their formative years as possible at home learning basic primary reading and counting skills from their parents rather than from strangers. This federal government education program is just another attempt to exercise more control over our children for a longer period of their childhood and start the government indoctrination process earlier in their lives.

The reason this belief originally became so popular dates back decades ago when feminist organizations started their protests against women being forced to stay at home with their children. They said that women were denied the same career choices as men because of this lifestyle. If women choose to have babies and a career, there should be prior discussion within the marriage about who stays at home with them. A neutral decision should then be reached based on priority. In some situations, the husband should stay at home; in others, the wife should.

Once you assume this difficult responsibility, you must live up to its challenge. It is not my intention to speak against the childcare daycare industry, but the children become the victims of a self-indulgent choice, not the adults. You can never be fully liberated from your bad choices until you take responsibility for them.

Malcolm X once said, "The final conflict in America will not be between people of different colors, but between people of different classes." He also said, "The building strength of a nation begins with the woman, because the mother is the first teacher of the child, and the message she gives to that child, she gives to the world."

For daughters, that message should be to choose a husband to be her child's father, and this message should be taught by example. What would this mean for the future of black America? For one thing, as I mentioned above, it strongly determines which side of the class line blacks will be on. Brother Malcolm also told us that, "If you are black and still follow the democrat party, you are a political fool, a flunky, and a traitor to your race."

Dr. King dreamed of an America that would not judge his children by the color of their skin but by the content of their character. If we do not prevent this oncoming cultural catastrophe, there soon will be no black people left in American with any integrity or character.

When blacks originally left Africa by force, our pedigree was damaged but not destroyed. After slavery, we rebuilt a new culture as proud black Americans. What we are doing now by our own actions is killing off our pedigree and our culture. Once this happens, it will be lost forever.

When we as black people allow our culture to gradually deteriorate to the point that 90 percent or more of our children are raised by unmarried women, we will then be a decayed population of criminals and dysfunctional misfits. Once the black American populace has geometrically regressed to a level of underachievers, the remaining generations of a criminal element will eventually eliminate each other with more black against black criminal violence?

Some decades after that, blacks will all but vanish from the North American continent as did the Native Americans. Then not only will black culture become extinct, the black man will become extinct as well.

In the 1940s, a black physician named Dr. Charles Drew discovered and developed the medical procedure of preserving and transfusing blood. Sometime later, tragic circumstances caused him to become in need of a transfusion, but he died from lack of such a medical procedure. A simple blood transfusion would have saved his life, which means he died from the lack of his own invention.

This was a tragic irony. Dr. Drew made one of the most important scientific discoveries in medical history, and we can only speculate about what other discoveries he might have made had he lived.

There is another double entendre here: Dr. Drew's life and death were connected to the life-saving properties of human blood, yet we black people are committing a cultural genocide on our own bloodline. The life and possible death of black American culture is connected to the future preservation and integrity of our lineage and bloodline.

Just as Charles Drew died before his time, black American culture may die prematurely before it reaches full potential in its contribution to the greatness of America and the world.

How many future inventors and discovers have we already lost to that more than 70 percent growing up outside a traditional family structure? Where will our next generation of scientist, architects, pilots, military leaders, and other positive role models come from? They most definitely will not result from the present crop we will soon be harvesting. As I said earlier, most of America's great black leaders were products of strong two-parent families.

These are the people who were the descendants of great African warriors and leaders, people of true pedigree. We have been free from slavery for over 150 years; black people have more to achieve in this country. We have more important things to do than merely become filthy-mouthed rappers and spoiled athletes. We have not yet reached our full destiny as a people, and we will not if we destroy our own culture before it reaches total fruition. We have to hang onto our families. Not doing so has painful consequences in more ways than one.

My father and I loved each other very much, but our relationship had its share of problems because of the anger and painful resentment I buried inside myself for so many years. I had these feelings because my involvement with him was so rare when I was a boy; his father was likewise almost totally absent from his life when he was a child. The few times we did spend together were great because he was a good man and an affectionate father, but those times were too few. When I was about sixteen and my mother could no longer control my bad behavior, she forced me to live with him. It helped, but by that time, the damage was already done to my undisciplined psyche.

From that time on, there was a constant ebb and flow in our relationship. Some years, we were very close, and other years, our relationship was more volatile. After a long and protracted illness, my father, Terry Harrison, died on April 3, 2005, the day after Pope John Paul II died and the date before Dr. Martin Luther King Jr. was murdered.

My father had no religious affiliation, but I am Catholic. While I have always been quite skeptical about tales of the supernatural celestial spiritual afterlife, to this day, I wonder if this was some type of strange coincidence or perhaps God's method of letting my father send me a message from his new home of metaphysical dimension to give me some closure and peace with the regrets and problems of our relationship.

Also, I was born on Friday the thirteenth. My mother-in-law, Hennie Sadler, was buried on my forty-first birthday in 1998; and my father-in-law, Andrew Sadler Sr., was buried on the same day in 1999. Again, I wonder if this was some type of strange spiritual coincidence. Due to my dysfunctional childhood, I have always been less than enthusiastic about the celebration of my birthday, but because of the circumstance surrounding the passing of my in-laws who always expressed great love and affection for me, I now have a more grateful appreciation for my birthday than I ever had before.

I'd like to close not with fear but with the example of a couple of black men whose characters and behavior stood the test of time. One is Henry O. Flipper, the first black man to attend West Point Military Academy in the 1870s. What a tribute to courage!

Even more amazing was Christian Abraham Fleetwood, born in 1840, who became America's first black Civil War hero at only five feet four inches tall. His father was the senior steward for the sugar tycoon John C. Brune. The Brunes sent Fleetwood to college, and after graduation, he started the South's first black-owned newspaper called *The Lyceum Observer*. After that, he founded a local literary society called the Galbraith Lyceum.

In 1863, he enlisted in the Union army as a private and one week later was promoted to sergeant major. A year later, because of his heroic performance in battle, every single officer he had served under petitioned the secretary of war to promote him to officer rank. This would have made him the army's first black officer, but the recommendation was denied. Instead, he was awarded the Medal of Honor for his bravery.

Fleetwood's strength and integrity did not allow this disappointment to discourage him. After the war, he took a job as a bank accountant in Washington DC. In 1881, he became senior clerk for the department of war, a position he held for the rest of his life. He also married. His wife was a nurse and schoolteacher, and they had two children.

During his time with the war department, Fleetwood started an organization of instruction and leadership for young black men interested in the military called the Washington Cadet Corps. In 1887, this corps was incorporated into the District of Columbia's National Guard and President Grover Cleveland commissioned Fleetwood to be major of the battalion.

In 1898, the Spanish American War began and Fleetwood again volunteered for service. All of his high commanders who remembered him from his Civil War days again recommended his promotion to colonel. But because he was black, this rank was again denied and Fleetwood was instead offered the rank of lieutenant.

Some years later, he gave a speech in Atlanta at its Cotton States Exposition Event. He spoke about recognizing the contributions of black soldiers to their country and never mentioned his own accomplishments. In 1914, he died as one of America's greatest military heroes.

I could be wrong, because there are exceptions to every rule, but I would be willing to gamble we would not be surprised at how well the children, grandchildren, and great-grandchildren of Christian Abraham Fleetwood probably turned out. The 1800s provided a hostile environment for black people in America, but as the example of this fine man demonstrates, children develop properly when they have consistent daily exposure to the balance of normal behavior with both a male and female parent in the home, even under those threatening conditions.

There are lessons in behavior that children can only learn from their mother because she is female. Likewise, even the best mother is not qualified to teach children lessons in the example of male behavior.

The cerebral process of male and female behavior is hard-wired inside each of us and requires interaction with both male and female parents. For example, if you give a three-year-old boy a toy baby doll to play with and a three-year-old girl a football, the little boy will throw the doll and the little girl will pretend to feed the football while talking to it.

These children grow up into young women and men and eventually become attracted to each other. A man becomes attracted to a woman with the fantasy that her perfection will never change. However, as time passes, women inevitably change as a process of their further growth into womanhood. A woman becomes attracted to a man with the fantasy that his imperfections will change because of her presence in his life. But men usually don't change because their growth into manhood is more physical than emotional. Inside, most of us males are those little boys who still want to throw that football we now watch being thrown on TV. This is just another part of the difference between the two genders.

Men and women look, think, and act differently because they are different from each other. A child's exposure to the combination of healthy adult male and female behaviors develops a psychologically healthy child. We cannot continue to manufacture generations of fatherless children whose capacity for love and trust is crippled at birth and who inevitably perpetuate a dysfunctional cycle. We simply have to get back to the two-parent family structure as the status quo, not the exception it has become.

My obvious physical appearance indicates that my ancestral background is African, but because of the advanced state of our present DNA technology, my research has revealed a more detailed breakdown of my own pedigree. I have recently discovered that I am 90 percent African (53 percent Nigerian, 12 percent Ghanaian, 9 percent Congolese, and broken down small amounts of other African regions summing up to 16 percent), 9 percent European and 1 percent West Asian. Though I have great pride in this human biological ancestry that I share with millions of my black brothers and sisters, we as a people have a responsibility and obligation to future generations to restore and preserve our social, cultural, and spiritual pedigree as well. I criticize our behavior, but my message comes from a deep love for my people. "A great civilization is not conquered from without until it has destroyed itself from within" (Will Durant).

My grandfather, Arthur Gasaway, was a successful, self-made businessman with only a fifth grade education. When I was a boy of eleven years old, he once told me that the two worst things you could be in America is a colored man without his own business or a colored man without a college education. I believed him until now. I now realize the worst thing you can be in America is a colored man with a dying pedigree.

About the Author

MICHAEL HARRISON was born on the proverbial Friday the 13th in September 1957. He grew up in Atlanta, Georgia, with his divorced mother and two younger sisters and was primarily raised by his mother and two grandmothers with very little positive male influence in timidity.

By the time he was old enough to start public school, his mother was beginning her second marriage. Michael's grades declined early, and he showed signs of a learning disability. He speculates this may in part have been due to his parent's divorce and the violent physical abuse he and his mother endured at the hands of his stepfather, which he still recalls quite vividly.

Between his mother's second and third divorces, when he was eight years old, she convinced Michael's father that Michael might do better in parochial school. Although not a panacea, it often helps disturbed children somewhat.

During Michael's admittedly abhorrent teenage years, his mother sent him to live with his father, hoping that would be a solution. After graduating from Catholic high school in 1976, he attended two years of college but never graduated.

Michael entered the workforce while living an unstable lifestyle and occupied many different jobs until 1986. He then met his wife, Lynne, who came from a good home with seven children and two married parents. She was exactly what Michael was looking for, and the rest, as they say, is history. He and Lynne married in 1988 and have two daughters.

Printed in the USA
CPSIA information can be obtained
at www.ICGtesting.com
LVHW051045060224
771097LV00010B/35/J